CW01669055

SUCCESS IS INEVITABLE

17 LAWS TO UNLOCK YOUR HIDDEN POTENTIAL, SKYROCKET YOUR CONFIDENCE AND GET WHAT YOU WANT FROM LIFE

THIBAUT MEURISSE

© 2019 Thibaut Meurisse

All rights reserved. No portion of this book may be reproduced in any form without permission from the publisher, except as permitted by U.S. copyright law.

CONTENTS

Why Should You Read This Book?

Have you ever set a goal you failed to achieve? Now, imagine what would happen if you had the perfect understanding of how success works and could rely on a set of specific rules to help you achieve any goal in any area of your life? Excited yet?

Often, the reason people fail to achieve their wildest goals and fail to live the life they want long term is their lack of understanding of how success works. Having no clear map to guide them, they feel lost in the sea of information, unable to identify exactly what they need to do to reach their goals. This misunderstanding leads them to live far below their potential and accomplish far less than they otherwise could.

This book will help you gain a crystal-clear understanding of how success works and will provide the tools and the habits to help you develop the mindset you require to achieve your goals in every aspect of your life.

You will greatly benefit from this book if you recognize yourself in one or more of the following statements:

- You want to understand how success works in order to achieve any future goal.
- You want to master each area of your life and design the life you desire within the next few years.
- You want to make a living from your passion—whatever that may be.

If any of the above statements apply to you, order a copy of this book and start your personal transformation today.

How to Use This Book

I encourage you to read all the way through this book at least once. After that, I invite you to revisit the book and focus on the section(s) you want to explore in greater depth.

In this book, I include a number of exercises. Although I don't expect you to work through them all, I hope you will choose your favorites and apply them in your life. Remember, the results you obtain from this book depend on how much time and effort you're willing to invest.

If you feel this book could be of any use to your family members or friends, make sure you recommend it to them.

Your Free Step-By-Step Action Guide

To help you attain your goals I've created a free action guide. You can download an electronic version at the following URL or use the action guide available at the end of this book.

http://whatispersonaldevelopment.org/success-is-inevitable

If you have any difficulties downloading the action guide, contact me at:

thibaut.meurisse@gmail.com and I will send it to you as soon as possible.

INTRODUCTION

What if you could live your life as though success was inevitable? What if you knew with absolute certainty you would achieve most of your goals no matter how many times you fail along the way? How would that change the way you think, feel and act every day?

This is the concept I invite you to explore in this book.

The truth is, when it comes to transforming your life, your belief in yourself and in your vision is far more powerful than anything else. Extraordinary people don't become that way because they are geniuses; they are often ordinary people with an extraordinary mindset and a desire to fulfill their destiny no matter what obstacles may stand in their way. Successful individuals hold themselves to a high standard and see themselves for what they could become, not what they currently are. They maintain the vision of a compelling future where they are confident, happy and successful. And more importantly, they *believe*. Successful people believe they can achieve the results they want in each area of their lives whether it is their career, their relationships, their finance or their health.

World famous guru, Tony Robbins, says that in any interaction, people who display the most certainty have the most influence over the other(s). And in many cases, this is true. Now, what if *you* could be the person with the most certainty? What if you could develop the rock-solid confidence that success is not only inevitable for you, but also for everybody around you?

This book invites you to do just that. **It invites you to live your life as though success is inevitable for you.**

In these pages, I'll challenge you to make that conviction your main focus until it becomes a rock-solid belief that affects everything you do. I want you to hold that belief and remind yourself of it as often as possible, whether it is when you wake up, take a shower, drive to work or go to sleep. I want you to develop a level of confidence and certainty you've never experienced before, and I want to help you *expect* success and happiness to manifest in your life.

Imagine how much better your life would be if you understood and felt that, at a deeper level and in the long term, success is inevitable for you.

What new actions would you take? How much more confident would you be throughout your day? With such a belief, how would your life change over the next six months? What about the next twelve months? The next decade?

Success is inevitable if you are willing to:

- **Take the time to identify what you really want**
- **Work hard on yourself** and transform your mindset
- **Work hard on your craft** and develop all the skills you need to achieve your goals
- **Get rid of all excuses** to the best of your ability and take one hundred percent responsibility for your life no matter how hard it may be.
- ***Never* give up, and**
- **Believe that success is inevitable.**

The point of this book is not just to tell you success is inevitable. It is to explain *why* this is the case. To do so, we'll discuss at length how success works, and I'll show you a specific model you can use to achieve your future goals in any area of your life.

In **Part I**, we'll define success. I will introduce you to the power of responsibility and you will discover why belief, clarity and passion are critical to your success. I will explain in detail how you can develop these qualities.

In **Part II**, you will learn how to use the power of commitment to achieve success. You will learn why being committed—and not merely interested—is one of the prime keys to changing your life.

In **Part III**, I will demonstrate why trusting the process is critical to long-term success. You will learn the laws of success and how to develop the mindset needed to achieve each of your goals.

In **Part IV**, we will discuss the importance of building emotional resilience. You will discover why controlling your emotions is incredibly important, and you will also learn how to do so effectively.

In **Part V**, we will see how you can relate to others in a way that will guarantee your long-term success.

Finally, in the **Bonus** section, you will discover the additional core beliefs you can develop to achieve success. You will be introduced to some of the most powerful beliefs that, when developed over time, will allow you to raise your game and achieve more than you can ever imagine.

Are you ready?

PART I

MASTERING THE FOUR POWERS THAT ENABLE SUCCESS

1

SUCCESS IS A MINDSET

> The greatest discovery of all time is that a person can change his future by merely changing his attitude
>
> — Oprah Winfrey, host of the Oprah Winfrey Show

Success is a mindset. Working hard isn't enough. Unless you develop the mindset required to achieve your vision, you'll probably never turn your vision into a reality. To achieve extraordinary results, you need to develop an extraordinary mindset. Developing such a mindset requires you to utilize the four fundamental powers for success:

1. Responsibility
2. Belief
3. Clarity, and
4. Passion

If you picture success as a pyramid, the power of responsibility is its foundation on which everything else rests. The second layer is made up of three blocks: the power of belief, the power of clarity and the power of passion.

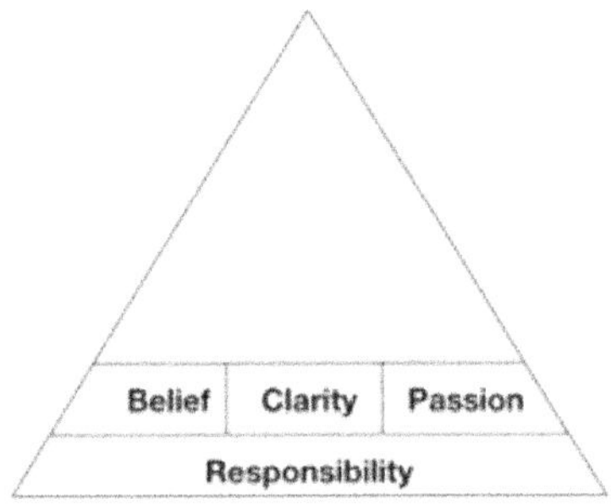

Defining success

Before I talk in greater detail about success and before I introduce the power of belief, clarity and passion, I will define what I mean by success.

Though money may be part of it, success is not solely defined in terms of the size of your bank balance. Being rich and famous doesn't necessarily guarantee you a happy life. Many wealthy people live miserable lives. In fact, you're probably better off than many rock stars or movie stars you might look up to.

Before we go further, I want you to develop your own definition of success. Too often, we fail to realize the extent our definition of success has been influenced by society or by our family and friends. It is extremely important you take a step back and ask yourself what you *really* want from life. You must do this with brutal honesty. Don't worry, you don't have to share your definition of success with anybody else. Feel free to go wild.

I define success as living life on my own terms. That is, doing something I love, surrounded by people I love, while having the money and/or time to do the things I want. After all, isn't that what everyone looks for?

For you, success might mean working only twenty-five hours a week to allow yourself plenty of time to dedicate to your hobbies and/or family (even if this means making less money). Alternatively, success could mean working sixty hours a week or more doing something you really enjoy and, in doing so, making good money so you can afford the things you want.

So, how you would define success? Are you living up to that definition right now?

* * *

Action step

Write down your personal definition of success using the free **Action Guide** (*Part I. Mastering the Four Powers That Enable Success*).

2

THE POWER OF ABSOLUTE RESPONSIBILITY

> Take full responsibility for what happens to you. It's one of the highest forms of human maturity ... It's the day you know you have passed from childhood to adulthood.
>
> — Jim Rohn, motivational speaker.

The key to achieving anything you want and to making your success inevitable is to take absolute and total responsibility for your life. This is by far the most powerful thing you can do to change your life. You must accept responsibility for all your actions and accept that you are mainly where you are because of who you are and what you do.

If you want to be somewhere else five years from now, how you think and the way you act will have to change. Your core belief will have to change. What you do every day will have to change.

As you start thinking and acting differently—and I cannot stress this highly enough—you cannot fail to alter the course of your destiny. Remember, human beings are the only species on earth with the power to design the future they want to live in.

Why taking responsibility is critical

People like to blame others or bad luck for their situation in life. And sometimes, it is undeniable that an event or situation may have been caused by external factors, at least to some extent.

No wonder the urge to blame external factors can be so strong, especially when these same external factors might be partially responsible for your life circumstances. The real meaning of taking responsibility, however, has nothing to do with apportioning blame or being right. You're not looking at who is to blame for a particular situation. You're not searching for a culprit.

To be honest, it doesn't matter who was right and who was wrong *in the past*. To achieve success *in the future*, you need to take one hundred percent responsibility for your life right now.

It's about taking absolute control over your life so you can achieve anything you've ever wanted to achieve. It's about reclaiming the power to transform your life. It's about making your long-term success and happiness an absolute priority.

As we'll see in more depth with *The Law of Humility*, your ability to set aside your ego and take responsibility for your life will greatly improve the results you achieve in every area of life.

Without responsibility no change is possible

The more responsibility you take for your life, the more power you have to change it. This is a universal law.

Why is this the case?

Imagine you're in an unsatisfying relationship. Naturally, you believe your partner is wrong while you're mostly, if not completely and consistently, right. In such a situation, how much power do you think you have to improve the relationship?

Since you believe you're not responsible for the quality of the relationship, not much.

Now, what if you were to take one hundred percent responsibility for your relationship? How much power would you have to change it?

Perhaps you could listen to your partner's complaints, determine whether there is some truth there and do something about it. Perhaps you could ask your partner what you could do better. Perhaps you could express the way you feel, instead of hiding your resentment. Or perhaps you could choose to separate if it's obvious the relationship is not working and has no chance of working in the future. As you accept full responsibility, the choices you can make dramatically increase. Also, the more options you have, the more power you have to change your life situation.

Taking extra responsibility

Taking absolute responsibility for your life means you're willing to accept as much responsibility as you possibly can.

Let's imagine you delegate a task to someone and the job isn't done properly. Your first reaction might be to blame the person for his or her incompetence. Instead, you should ask yourself, "How could I be responsible in this situation?" For instance, perhaps you asked the wrong person to complete the task. Maybe you didn't give them the right instructions. Or you may have failed to follow-up and monitor the progress of the project. As you can see, even in this specific situation you are responsible for the outcome of the task.

In fact, when you trace a problem back to its origins, you'll often find you could have avoided it if you had taken more care. Maybe you could have taken more time to plan or could have asked for advice. Or maybe you could have been less complacent. To address this issue, I encourage you to work through the following exercise:

1. Look at one thing that currently bothers you—the challenge.
2. Go back in time and try to find the root cause.
3. Then, decide what you could have done differently to prevent the challenge from happening in the first place.

By completing this exercise, you may realize how much overall responsibility you had for the outcome. One benefit of taking extra responsibly is that you will become better at anticipating problems. As you regularly ask yourself, "How am I responsible here," you will train your mind to look for ways to think and act differently. This, in turn, will allow you to prevent similar problems from happening in the future (e.g., asking the wrong person to do a task in the first instance).

Accepting what you can't change

Taking absolute responsibility also entails accepting things you cannot change. If you lose your legs in a car accident and end up in a wheelchair, you might not be able to do much about it, but you can accept your situation one hundred percent. The motivational speaker, Nick Vujicic was born with no arms or legs. As you can imagine, he was angry about his situation for years. He thought he would never be able to find a job or get married like "normal" people. He could have remained bitter for his entire life, but at some point, he decided to accept his disabilities and make the most of his challenges. He then became a successful motivational speaker and a father of two. Now that is what I call a real success story.

The bottom line is you are responsible for how you react to life's events. Blaming others won't help you. The blame game will only succeed in making you unhappy.

What about you? How would your situation change if you decided to take one hundred percent responsibility for your life?

Now, look at each area of your life. How could you improve each one by taking absolute responsibility for them?

Take more responsibility for your life than anybody else and you'll see that, in the long run, your life will dramatically improve. Remember, nothing in your life can change until you do. If your life is going to change, the change will have to start with you.

* * *

Action step

Using your **Action Guide**, answer the following question: What is the one thing you could start doing today to get better results in one particular area of your life? (*Section I. The Power of Absolute Responsibility*).

3

THE POWER OF BELIEF

> If you limit your choices only to what seems possible or reasonable, you disconnect yourself from what you truly want, and all that is left is a compromise.
>
> — Robert Fritz, author of The Path of Least Resistance.

The ability to believe is one of the most fundamental components of success. It opens the door to limitless possibilities and allows you to turn all your dreams and desires into reality. Belief enables you to develop your skills, abilities and talents to the highest degree possible, and it helps you make your biggest contribution to the world.

Your level of belief in yourself and in your overall vision acts as a filter to determine what you can and cannot do in life. Lack of self-belief erodes your potential and severely reduces what you can accomplish. As Henry Ford once said, "*Whether you think you can, or you think you can't—you're right.*"

Failing to believe in something almost automatically removes that thing from your reality, making it almost impossible for it to manifest in your life. For instance:

- If you believe you can't find the job you love, you'll never design a career you're passionate about.
- If you believe you can't improve, you'll continue to live far below your potential.
- If you believe you can't develop a healthy self-esteem, you'll live the rest of your life with low self-confidence, which will negatively affect your well-being and your potential. It could even prevent you from attracting your ideal partner or designing a meaningful career.

We *must* believe in something before we can see it. It doesn't work the other way around. This is what makes human beings different from every other animal on the planet. We can use our imagination to turn the invisible—an idea—into the visible. With strong belief, we can have a tangible result in the real world.

Unfortunately, most people struggle to reach a level of belief that will allow them to transform their life. Instead, they search for leaders and gurus to tell them how to think and behave. Psychological experiments have shown how easily we can be influenced.

For instance, the Milgram experiment revealed how most people blindly obey individuals perceived as authority figures—in the Milgram test, this was the man with a white coat. In this well-known experiment, participants were led to believe they were administering electric shocks to "students" to study how people learn. The real purpose of the experiment, however, was to see how participants would react to orders when it went against their conscience. In many cases, the participants blindly followed the so-called doctor's orders, even when the "students" (who were, in fact, actors) explicitly demanded they stop, mentioning a heart problem. In short, under the instructions or commands of the so-called doctor, many participants were willing to endanger the lives of the "students" rather than disobey orders from an authority figure.

The Asch conformity experiments is another example of how easily people can be influenced. In these experiments, a group of participants were each given two cards; one card displayed a single line, the other showed three lines, A, B and C, each of different lengths. The group of participants was, in turn, asked to say aloud which of the three lines on the second card (A, B or C) matched the length of the line on the first card. Among the eight participants, seven were actors and only one was the actual participant. In this experiment, the actual participants gave wrong answers 36.8% of the time (as opposed to 1% of participants in the control group, without the actors).

After seeing the majority giving incorrect answers one after the other, some participants concluded that the majority must have been right. In short, they knew the correct answers, but didn't have the confidence to contradict the group majority.

These two classic and well-cited experiments show how our lack of self-belief can lead us to make wrong and even harmful decisions under the pressure of a single authority figure or a group of people.

While these are only experiments, they reflect how society works. Society tends to act as an invisible force that pulls us toward mediocrity. The authority figures (our parents, teachers and the media) and our peers (friends and colleagues) constantly remind us our goals are impossible, and thereby dissuade us from pursuing our dreams successfully.

If you put a group of crabs in a bucket, none of them will survive. Whenever a crab tries to escape, others will grab it and drag it back down. As you climb your way toward greatness, you may feel as though you are trying to escape from a bucket, with everyone pulling you back. This is especially true if you happen to live in a toxic environment with no successful role model to look up to.

In truth, you will certainly fail to achieve your goals many times, but this is how you grow and learn. Through repeated "failures" you'll learn from your mistakes and end up achieving far more than you can ever imagine. This is how your mind works. Unfortunately, most people will never reach this stage because they don't believe in themselves enough to dare to fail enough times. As a result, they give up too soon.

To succeed in life, you must learn to develop an unshakable belief in yourself and in your vision. You need to reach a point where your self-belief exceeds the lack of belief other people have in you and in your vision. Whenever possible, you should avoid spending time with negative people who do not believe in you or your ultimate success—they will only drag you back down into the bucket of obscurity.

How to believe in yourself and in your vision

In his book, *6 Months to 6 Figures,* Peter Voogd wrote, "*There is nothing more powerful than self-confidence in multiplying your income by two, by three, by five, and then by ten.*"

Think about this for a moment. What if Peter Voogd is correct? How magical would that be?

Self-confidence is one of the key factors to success. In this section, we'll see how to develop a rock-solid belief in yourself and in your vision.

My friend, Mike Pettigrew, author of *The Most Powerful Goal Achieving System in the World*, explains how his low level of self-esteem directly impacted his business and his life. His business was losing money, primarily because he priced his service too low. Facing bankruptcy, he doubled his prices. Surprisingly, none of his customers left. In fact, some of them even told him his services had been too cheap in the first place. What do you think his main reason was for not charging enough money? Yes, that's right—it was his lack of self-confidence.

Self-confidence will not only affect your bank account, it will also affect other areas of your life. Low self-confidence may prevent you from going after the job you really want. It may stop you from asking out the person you like. Finally, low self-confidence can make you feel bad about yourself.

No matter what your level of self-confidence is now, I'm about to show you how you can boost it to give yourself a better chance to create the life you really want.

The Self-Empowerment Triangle

For the most part, what you think, feel and do determines your level of confidence. When your thoughts, feelings and actions work together to create the identity of a highly confident person, your confidence will grow naturally and exponentially. In other words, success most definitely breeds success.

Unfortunately, we often fail to make the connection between self-discipline (what we do consistently), and self-esteem/self-confidence (how we think and feel about ourselves). Self-confidence and self-esteem are largely determined by our ability to complete and achieve our goals. The more self-discipline we develop, the more we respect ourselves and the more confident we feel as a result. This is what I call the *Self-Empowerment Triangle.*

The *Self-Empowerment Triangle* works as follows:

As we discipline ourselves to finish small tasks to the best of our ability (self-discipline), we feel better about ourselves (self-esteem). By repeatedly doing so, we learn to trust our ability to achieve our future goals (self-confidence).

Another key element required to make the *Self-Empowerment Triangle* work is self-compassion, which is the glue that binds self-discipline, self-confidence and self-esteem. Self-compassion enables self-empowerment and makes it durable. If we keep beating ourselves up whenever we "fail," our self-esteem and self-confidence will suffer. We'll talk about self-compassion in more detail in a separate section (see *Cultivating self-compassion*).

Now, for clarity sake, here is a brief definition of each of the elements constituting the *Self-Empowerment Triangle:*

- **Self-discipline:** the ability to do what you should do, when you should do it, whether you feel like it or not.
- **Self-esteem:** the respect you have for yourself.
- **Self-confidence:** the inner knowledge that you can cope effectively with life's challenges and, by doing so, you will achieve your goals.
- **Self-compassion:** the deep understanding that you're *exactly* where you're supposed to be at any given moment and that you have a total love and acceptance of the current situation.

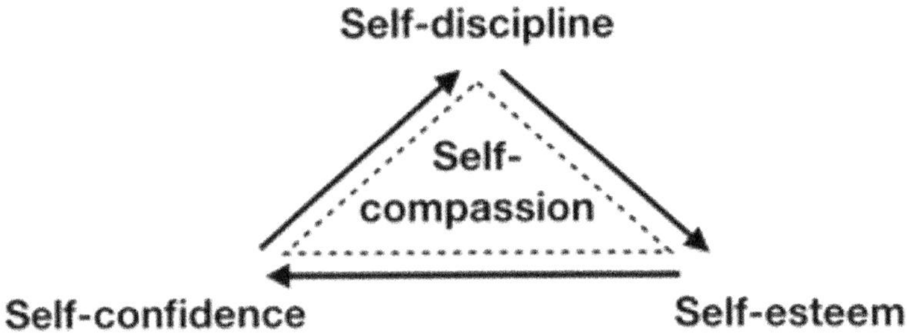

Self-Empowerment Triangle

Now, let's see how you can use the *Self-Empowerment Triangle* to generate success.

Building self-discipline

Your ability to do what you should do when you should do it, whether you feel like it or not, will, for the most part, determine your future success. To develop more self-discipline, you must start by completing small tasks consistently. As you do so, your self-esteem will grow, (see also **Part IV: Overruling your feelings**).

Fortunately, you don't have to start big. Consistency is more important than magnitude or intensity. By setting small, achievable goals you will find it easier to remain consistent over the years and therefore are more likely to be successful. Take New Year's Resolutions as an example. At the beginning of the year, the nation's gyms become crowded with new members who are inspired by their resolutions. A couple of months (or weeks) later, gyms are empty again and exercise classes return to their standard occupancy. Needless to say, setting large, unrealistic resolutions (goals) is not how to build confidence and achieve great results.

Rather than trying to accomplish massively ambitious tasks, choose a simple target and commit to completing it every day. Select a task linked to one of your major long-term goals. Perhaps you could complete a certain number of press-ups every morning. Or maybe you could jog a certain distance. Alternatively, you could write a specific number of words or read a few pages of your favorite inspirational book. Simply completing one simple thing each day will enhance your self-discipline and your self-confidence, and it will help make you feel better about yourself.

In my book, *Habits That Stick*, I offer a list of the seven most powerful habits you can adopt. These habits will have a profound impact on your life in the long run, and they include:

Setting daily goals

Setting your goals every single day will boost your productivity. To set your goals, take a pen and paper and make a list of three to five tasks you want to accomplish. Then, prioritize these tasks in order of importance. Complete your first task before moving on to the next one. Repeat the process until all the tasks are done.

Meditating

Meditation provides many benefits, which include:

- Reduced worry
- Enhanced self-esteem and self-acceptance
- Improved resilience against pain
- Heightened/Enriched mood
- Increased focus, and
- Improved blood pressure.

If you want to learn more, check out the article the following article: http://liveanddare.com/benefits-of-meditation. It mentions over seventy-six scientific benefits of meditation. There are many ways to meditate, but it can be as simple as closing your eyes and focusing on your breathing. You can begin by spending just a few minutes on this each day.

Practicing gratitude

Practicing gratitude is a powerful way to enhance your overall happiness. To learn how to cultivate gratitude refer to the section, *Practicing Gratitude* in **Part IV**.

Consuming motivational books and videos

No matter how exciting your goals may be, there will be times when you won't feel like doing anything. Feeding your mind with inspirational material on a daily basis will help you stay motivated for the long haul.

Daily exercise

Studies have shown that moderate exercise has a positive impact on both your physical and mental health. According to research published in PLoS Medicine, two and a half hours moderate exercise each week could add more than three years to your lifespan. As for the benefits of exercising on your mood, they are both immediate and long term. Professor of psychology, Michael Otto, says people usually derive a mood-enhancement effect within five minutes of partaking in moderate exercise.

To learn more about the power of mini-habits, check out Stephen Guise's book, *Mini-Habits.*

* * *

Action step

Write down one thing you could start doing consistently every day for the next thirty days. And then, most importantly, *do it*! (*Part II. The Power of Belief*)

How to boost your self-esteem

As you adopt one simple daily habit and stay consistent with it, you will boost your self-esteem. This is one of the main reasons daily self-discipline is so important.

How often have you felt guilty because you didn't do what you planned to do? This is when self-compassion is so valuable. A healthy dose of self-compassion is far more powerful in helping you stay on track with your goal than constant self-criticism. In the section, *Cultivating Self-Compassion*, we will learn about the concept in greater depth. We will also learn what you can do to cultivate self-compassion.

Additionally, self-discipline helps you build momentum. Have you ever felt good after completing a task you have been delaying for a while? And, after completing the chore, didn't it make you want to tackle similar tasks? This is known as the power of momentum.

However, developing more self-discipline is only one way to boost your self-esteem. Below are a few effective ways to enhance your self-esteem:

Acknowledge your small wins. While things may not always go as planned, we can choose to focus on all the things we're doing well. This is what confident people do. They blow their own horn, if you will. Conversely, people with little self-confidence tend to dwell on their failures. No wonder they feel inadequate. How about you? Do you acknowledge your small wins?

Reinterpreting your past. Instead of focusing on negative events, make sure you remember events that make you feel good and ignore all the negative ones. You'll notice that the things you refuse to focus on no longer exist and, from your mind's perspective, this is absolutely true. The less you think about something, the less power it has to generate negative feelings. And if you think that this is "cheating" please note, the human mind does this naturally. We tend to embellish past memories and often end up fantasizing about them. We remember how happy we were, dismissing all the little things that annoyed us at the time. This is a healthy process. You can take the same process one step further by consciously remembering positive events and discarding negative ones. Or you can give past events an entirely new meaning as I'll demonstrate in the next point.

Reframing your past. You can choose to interpret your past differently. Rather than focusing on your mistakes, learn to show compassion toward your younger self and acknowledge your noble intentions. Realize your past is not set in stone, at least not in the way our brain interprets it. After all, we only remember fragments of our past, and we filter these memories based on our own changing belief system and self-image. As David J. Schwartz wrote in his excellent book, *The Magic of Thinking Big, "Much lack of self-confidence can be traced directly to a mismanaged memory."* As you learn to manage your memory better, your self-esteem will naturally grow alongside it.

Here are some practical exercises to boost your self-esteem:

1. **What three things do you want to acknowledge yourself for?** They can be simple things such as eating healthily, helping a friend or waking on time. The idea is to learn to focus on the things you're doing well.

Another quick tip: make sure you acknowledge yourself for the things that matter to you. For instance, I dread administrative tasks and it can sometimes take me weeks just to fill in a form that requires a few minutes to complete. I like to celebrate these types of accomplishments because they are meaningful to *me.*

2. **Write down all your accomplishments.** Don't be shy, write down all your past accomplishments—small and big. This exercise works best when done once in a while. After you have done so, allow yourself to feel proud of these past accomplishments. Mix them together and, if it helps, listen to songs that elicit feelings of gratitude while doing so.

3. **Reward yourself.** Make sure you celebrate every important milestone. For instance, I celebrate each time I release a new book. I also set specific rewards for major goals. Ideally, the reward should be something you genuinely want. It could be going out for dinner, eating your favorite cake or buying a long-awaited book.

4. **Record every positive thing people have said about you.** In a journal, write down all the positive things people tell you. For instance, it could be a compliment your colleagues give you on your hairstyle. Or it could be something nice your spouse tells you. This process will train you to look for the positives in your daily life. I created such a journal a few years ago and go through it on a regular basis, updating it whenever necessary.

These two things alone—developing self-discipline and acknowledging your small wins—will go a long way in increasing your self-esteem. The key is to be consistent.

* * *

Action step

Complete at least one of the four exercises above using the **Action Guide** (*Section II. The Power of Belief*).

Building self-confidence

The daily discipline of achieving small tasks and acknowledging your wins will boost your self-confidence over the long term. And the more confident you become, the more likely you are to achieve your goals which will, in turn, further enhance your confidence. I consider this one of my virtuous circles.

Understanding success

Learning about the mechanism of success will allow you to develop even more confidence, which is what this book is mainly about. It will make you realize that success is inevitable through a clear understanding of how success works. As you build a better mental representation of the process called "success," you will feel far more confident in your ability to achieve your goals long term.

Having integrity

Another key to building deeper self-confidence and self-respect is having integrity in everything you do. This means telling the truth to yourself and to others and doing what you know is right. This implies knowing your core values, beliefs and personality traits and being able to identify your strengths and the areas of interest you wish to pursue. We'll talk about that in more detail in the following sections when we discuss the power of clarity and passion.

Finally, remember you can learn to believe in yourself. Nobody is born with self-confidence and self-belief. Confidence is something you acquire over time. Thus, if you've been struggling with confidence issues, don't assume anyone but you can build self-confidence because of X, Y or Z. You *can* become more confident and you *will*. In fact, like success, self-confidence is inevitable. There is no reason you can't develop more self-confidence in the long term.

By now, you should understand why believing in something is critical in helping you achieving anything you want in life.

* * *

Action step

Complete the corresponding exercises in the **Action Guide** (*Section II. The Power of Belief*).

4

THE POWER OF CLARITY

> It's a lack of clarity that creates chaos and frustration. Those emotions are poison to any living goal.
>
> — Steve Maraboli, motivational speaker and author.

The third step to creating a successful life is to know exactly what you want. In his excellent book, *High Performance Habits*, Brendon Burchard identifies "seeking clarity" as one of the six fundamental habits used by high achievers. It sounds obvious, but you cannot fulfill a vision you don't have. Most people achieve mediocre results simply because they don't really know what they want. These people wake up every day with no clear objective. They have no goal for the year. Neither do they have a specific vision for each area of their lives. As a result, they get no closer to their ideal life.

But why wander through life hoping for success when you can decide exactly what you want and take positive daily action to make your vision a reality?

Remember, you can use your imagination to design the life you want, and this is what differentiates you from any other living thing on earth.

Creating a clear picture of your ideal future is critical. You *must* seek clarity to design a better future. You must work on refining your vision continuously by asking yourself, "What do I really want?"

Once you have determined your life goal, it becomes easier to focus your time, effort and resources on the desired outcome. Instead of being "all over the place," you will be able to zero-in on your vision and act with laser-sharp focus. This, in turn, will stop you wasting time on trivial tasks and will significantly increase your performance and improve your ultimate chance of success.

The bottom line is that wanting to make more money, to be successful or to be happy aren't goals. They are merely wishes or fantasies. You must become crystal clear and define what you want as specifically as possible. For instance:

- Exactly how much money do you want to make?
- What does success look like to you?
- What does happiness mean to you?

Unless you can answer these questions, you risk spending most of your life chasing the wrong things. To avoid this outcome, make sure you know who you are and what you want from life.

1. Defining what you want

The best way to identify what you want is to have an honest look at each area of your life. How close are you to your ideal in the following areas of your life? Consider the following aspects:

- **Career/mission:** do you wake up excited about your goals? Do you feel as though you're making a difference in your own unique way?
- **Family:** do you spend enough quality time with your family?
- **Finance:** do you make enough money to do what you want in life or do you struggle to make ends meet?
- **Health (Physical):** do you have a healthy body?

- **Health (Emotional):** how good is your emotional wellbeing?
- **Personal growth:** do you feel as though you're growing into the person you want to become?
- **Relationship:** is your relationship with your partner the best it could be?
- **Spirituality:** do you feel a sense of connection with God/the universe?

Rank yourself on a scale of 1 to 10 for each of the areas above, where 1 means you are miles away from your ideal, and 10 means you have it exactly the way you want.

Now for each area, take a few minutes to visualize in detail what your ideal vision looks like. See yourself as being already at a 10 in each area and answer the following questions:

- **Career:** what contribution are you making to society and the world in general? What does your day at work look like?
- **Family:** how are you interacting with your family on a day-to-day basis and how does that make you feel?
- **Finance:** how much money are you earning each month? What are you doing with this money?
- **Health:** how do you feel every day? What does your diet look like?
- **Personal growth:** what three words best describe you? What do you think people say about you when you're not there? What message are you spreading to the world?
- **Relationship:** what emotions are you experiencing daily? How do you treat your partner? And how do they feel as a result? How does your partner treat you?
- **Spirituality:** how do you serve God or the universe? What spiritual qualities do you embody?

If you can define what you want in each area of your life, you're already ahead of most people.

Writing down what you want

Now you have defined what you want in each area of your life, let's try to be even more specific. Remember, *clarity is power*. For each area, write down a short statement that defines how your ideal self feels, thinks and acts. This represents your vision for each specific area.

Below are two tips to help you design an effective vision statement.

1. It must be inspiring when you read it. Write something that resonates with you and that motivates you to take action. Make your statement as short and concise as possible.
2. You must be able to visualize the outcome. Add specific visions to give your statement more power. What are you doing? Who are you surrounded by? How do you feel?

Here are some examples of vision statements:

Career/mission:

I wake up every day with a clear purpose and a deep sense of responsibility. I have an unshakable belief in myself, an unwavering commitment to change people's lives, and my love for others allows me to transform countless people's lives.

Finance:

I create wealth. I manifest abundance in my life by serving people all around me and inspiring them to become the best they can be. I can buy all the things I need, do all the things I want, and become all I can become.

Health:

My body is my temple. Every day I nourish it with incredibly healthy foods that give me abundant energy to take care of my family, do amazing work and make each day memorable. I'm excited about living a long, happy and healthy life, savoring each moment with a deep sense of gratitude and love. The healthier I am, the happier I become.

Personal growth:

I'm totally confident in my ability to achieve anything I want. Every day, I become better, stronger and wiser. By who I've become, I inspire everybody around me to be who they've always wanted to be. I'm overcoming my fears and limitations so I can love more, live more and serve more. My compassion toward myself and others has no limit. My determination to be all I can be has no boundary. I am unlimited potential and pure love.

These are merely examples. The key is to make sure your vision statement inspires you. The more you imbue it with your values and use words that strike powerful chords, the better.

For instance, if you want to become healthier, you have to determine why it matters to you. You can sometimes pursue the right goal for the wrong reasons. While your focus may be on losing weight, what you really want is to stay healthy until old age so you can watch your great-grand children grow. This simple reframing can help boost your motivation and increase your likelihood of success.

This isn't an easy exercise so don't worry about coming up with the perfect vision statement. You can always refine it over time and will probably need to do so as you evolve over the years. At this stage, having some clarity is far better than having none at all.

Knowing your core values

Unless you know what drives you deep down, you'll have a hard time designing a life you truly enjoy. What do you value most? Truth? Freedom? Relationships? Learning? Creativity?

What are values?

Values aren't things you believe you should do because society or your family said so, but they are what you're naturally drawn towards. For instance, perhaps you have a love for learning, a yearning for truth or a craving for more freedom.

Think of your core values as the principles that determine whether you live your life with integrity. That is, whether you're acting every day as, deep down, you know you should. When you fail to act with integrity, you'll experience resistance and suffering. This is usually a sign you're not living up to your true values.

Of course, we all have many values that are important to us. The key to success, however, is to identify those which are truly the most important.

Take a few minutes to write down your top ten core values. Again, don't try to come up with the perfect answers, simply trust your intuition and write down what feels right to you at this moment.

The importance of self-awareness

Cultivating self-awareness, defined as "the ability to learn about yourself every day and self-reflect," is essential to help you identify who you are and what you want. It is difficult to live a great life without true self-awareness. While you may have a seemingly successful career, without self-awareness, you run the risk of living an unfulfilled life that fails to reflect your core values or personality. Here are some examples of what self-awareness encompasses:

Being able to identify your core values and live by them. Refer to the previous section on discussing values.

Knowing your weaknesses. Identify your weaknesses and find ways to cope with them. This could be by working on them, having someone else support you or simply ignoring them. Some weaknesses can act as bottlenecks that prevent you from reaching higher levels of success and happiness, while other weaknesses may be irrelevant (which is often the case). I recommend you work mostly on weaknesses that may prevent you from achieving your long-term visions—your bottlenecks—and ignore the others. Meanwhile, work on your strengths to become truly exceptional at what you're doing.

Understanding your core beliefs and the way they affect your behaviors and actions. Do you hold disempowering beliefs relating to money? Do you believe you can improve in any area you want (growth mindset) or do you believe you're doomed to stay at your current situation (fixed mindset)? Reading this book will allow you to develop new empowering beliefs, but only if you take action to change for the better.

Identifying the recurrent thought patterns that prevent you from reaching your potential. What negative emotions do you experience on a regular basis? Do you often think you're not good enough? Do you keep beating yourself up? If so, what major thoughts or circumstances trigger these patterns? A great exercise is to write down the emotions you experience during the day every night for a week. It will help you identify some of your most common thoughts and emotions.

Identify your "zone of genius," i.e., what you're doing better than anybody else. What are some of the things only you can do? Don't dismiss anything. Perhaps it is your incessant desire to learn. Perhaps it is your ability to influence people. Perhaps it is your exceptional memory. Seemingly unimportant strengths can make a huge difference in your life when you leverage them to the maximum. A great exercise to help you identify your strengths is to send an email to your family, friends and/or colleagues and simply ask them what they believe your particular strengths are. Another tip is to look at the tasks you find so easy you can't understand why other people find the same tasks difficult.

Knowing whether you're an extrovert or an introvert and understanding all the implications. The key difference between extroverts and introverts is in the way they recharge their batteries. Extroverts need to be around people and live in stimulating environments to feel energized. Introverts, on the other hand, feel most energized when they are in quiet environments by themselves or with a few people. To learn more about introversion, I invite you to refer to my book, *The Thriving Introvert: Embrace the Gift of Introversion and Live the Life You Were Meant to Live.*

Being able to monitor your emotions and avoid reacting mechanically. Your ability to control your emotions greatly determines your happiness and your overall performances. In **Part IV**, we'll discuss in great length what you can do to manage your emotions better. You can learn more about emotions in my book, *Master Your Emotions: A Practical Guide to Overcome Negativity and Better Manage Your Feelings.*

Identifying your blind spots and seeking new perspectives. You can easily get stuck in the same old paradigm of thinking and end up unable to see new perspectives. Take note of when you lose sight of the big picture and seek the help of people who can give you some perspective. This could be by hiring a coach or talking to a friend.

Being able to listen to your intuition. You're here to live *your* life, not the life other people want you to live. Your ability to listen to your intuition can be developed in different ways. For instance, you can start making decisions based on your intuition rather than doing what other people expect of you. You can also spend more time alone to reduce external influences, whether they be your family and friends or the media. Additionally, asking your subconscious mind questions such as, "What am I supposed to do?" or "What do I really want?" can also help. The best time to do this is before going to sleep, which is when your subconscious mind is most receptive.

Self-awareness leads to clarity. Realize that the cultivation of self-awareness is an on-going process and continuously seek clarity by identifying what matters most to you (your core value) and how you want to express yourself to the world (your purpose).

People who know exactly what they want to do tend to achieve far more than people with no clear vision. This is because they can move toward their vision with laser-sharp focus rather than scattering their energy.

* * *

Action step

Complete the corresponding exercises in the **Action Guide** to gain clarity on what you really want (*Section III. The Power of Clarity*).

2. Setting crystal clear goals

Gaining clarity regarding who you are and what you want to be or do happens at a macro level. You must also gain clarity at the micro level, by setting crystal clear and specific goals.

Most people only have vague goals. There are several reasons for this. One obvious reason is they don't know what they want. Another is probably that they have a fear of failure. After all, if they set a goal and fail to achieve it, they consider themselves a "failure." Yet another reason is that they were never taught how to set goals. Sadly, there is no course on goal setting at school. As a result, most people will graduate from school or university without having learned how to set clear goals and achieve them.

What goals are

Goals are desirable results you want to achieve at some time in the future. Ideally, they are aligned with your values and part of a bigger vision or purpose. Setting goals is like entering a destination into your GPS. Goal setting gives clarity and allows your subconscious mind to work on your goals 24/7. In the same way that you can't type the name of a city and expect to arrive at the specific address, you can't set an ill-defined goal of, say, making more money, being happy or losing weight and expect to achieve the tangible results you're after. You must know precisely what you want to achieve in order to create a plan and enable your subconscious mind to guide you.

Let's see how you can set goals effectively.

Setting SMART goals

You may be familiar with SMART goals, but it won't hurt to review the process quickly.

In this instance, "SMART" stands for:

- **Specific:** what exactly do you want? What are you trying to achieve?
- **Measurable:** can you assess the progress toward your goal easily? How will you know whether you've achieved it?
- **Achievable:** is the goal achievable? Is the timeframe realistic? Can you put in the effort required, despite your other responsibilities?
- **Relevant:** is the goal in line with your core values? Does it excite you?
- **Time-bound:** does your goal have a clear deadline?

Below is one example of SMART goals. It's actually one of the goals I set at the beginning of 2018.

My goal: I will complete eight books by December 31st, 2018.

- Is it specific? Yes, I have to write eight books within twelve months.
- Is it measurable? Yes, I can break down my goal into eight, six-week-long milestones, and make it easy to assess whether I'm on track.
- Is it achievable? Yes, I've been able to write books in short periods of time before, so I know I can do it again. I have the time and willingness to do so.
- Is it relevant? Yes, I like writing inspirational books. The goal is aligned with my mission of helping people become their best self.
- Is it time-bound? Yes, there is a clear deadline, which is December 31st, 2018.

You want your goals to be at least this specific.

Breaking down your goals

No matter how big your goal is, you can always break it down into smaller tasks. A yearly goal can be broken down into a 90-day goal, a monthly goal, a weekly goal and even a daily goal. For instance, a goal of writing eight books in one year can be divided into eight projects of smaller sub-tasks such as creating an outline, completing the first draft, completing the second draft, et cetera.

Then, for each goal, you can identify several key tasks you must work on every single day. Knowing what you have to do every day is invaluable as it sharpens your focus and makes it far more likely you'll achieve your long-term goal. We'll see how to identify key tasks in more detail in the upcoming section, *The Law of Effective Action.* In my case, an example of a key task would be writing every day.

Now you understand the importance of belief and have gained more clarity regarding who you are and what you want, let's look at the power of passion.

To learn how to set exciting goals and discover the SMART Goals Method in greater detail, I encourage you to refer to my book, *Goal Setting: The Ultimate Guide to Achieving Goals that Truly Excite You.*

* * *

Action step

Set at least one SMART goal and break it down in the **Action Guide** (*Section III. The Power of Clarity - Setting Crystal-clear Goals*).

5

THE POWER OF PASSION

> When you catch a glimpse of your potential, that's when passion is born.
>
> — Zig Ziglar, salesman and motivational speaker.

Are you passionate about what you're doing, or do you constantly rely on willpower alone to complete your tasks?

Highly successful people tend to be passionate, perhaps even obsessed, about what they're doing. They have a compelling vision, and they can't wait to make it happen. When you're deeply passionate about what you're doing, your chances of success long term are significantly increased. You have far more energy and enthusiasm, and you are able to persevere longer than the average person will. To paraphrase Steve Jobs, you must have a lot of passion for what you do because it's so hard, if you don't, any rational person would give up.

While there are heated debates on whether or not you should follow your passion, I believe that, to truly excel at what you do, you'll need to be extremely passionate about it.

As an example, I would probably have given up writing books a long time ago if I weren't obsessed about what I was doing. My level of obsession and my passion are the prime reasons you're able to read this book.

Defining passion

Before we explore the power of passion further, let's define what we mean by passion. While it can mean different things to different people, some of the following characteristics can be useful when trying to identify your specific passion as something that:

- **Naturally appeals to you:** when you're passionate about something, you're naturally drawn toward it. Look at what you're doing whenever you have free time. Are you losing track of time? That's a sign you're passionate.
- **Energizes you:** your passion should energize you. If you constantly have to motivate yourself, either your passion is not the right one for you, or it must be refined to energize you more effectively.
- **Stems from your life purpose:** a passion becomes even more powerful when it is linked to a broader mission or a life purpose. If your passion is impacting other people's lives in a positive way whether by entertaining them, helping them or touching them in some way, you might be onto something.

Now, let's have a look at six questions you can ask to help find your passion.

1. What did you enjoy doing when you were a young child? Often, what we do as kids reveals certain aspects of our personality. As time passes, we tend to become distracted by life (school, sport, work or even video games). When I was a kid I usedr to read a lot. Sometimes, I read most of the day. I even remember writing short stories when I was eight. Ironically, it took me more than twenty years to return to writing, and this is something I would never have predicted.

2. Who do you envy? What are the people you envy doing? I used to be jealous of successful personal development bloggers. I wanted to do the same thing they were doing.

3. If all your family members, friends and people you know were no longer around and you were completely alone, what would you start doing? This situation allows you to think about what you want to do in this world without worrying about familial or societal pressures.

4. If you had all the time and money in the world, what would you do? (After partying and drinking cocktails on the beach got boring!) This situation removes issues you might have, like lack of time and lack of money, and gives you an opportunity to think about what you want to do more creatively and without boundaries.

5. If you had complete confidence and were already your absolute best self, what would you be doing with your life? This helps you envision your best self and removes any sense of limiting fear. It can also help you find clarity on what you really want to do in life.

6. How do you want to express yourself to the world? Do you want to entertain, educate, inspire, heal, teach or create? What emotions do you want people to feel as a result of the work you're doing? This question helps you clarify your means of expression and how you want to serve the world.

Being passionate gives you tremendous energy and makes it far more likely you'll achieve your goals long term. However, passion is not the only tool to rely on when designing an exciting future. Another way to generate energy is to identify compelling reasons why your goal *must* become a reality.

To learn how to find your passion, I encourage you to read my book, *The Passion Manifesto: Escape the Rat Race, Uncover Your Passion, and Design a Career and Life You Love.*

* * *

Action step

Uncover your passion using the corresponding section of the **Action Guide** (*Section IV. The Power of Passion*).

Strengthening your "whys"

While passion motivates you to engage in a specific activity you enjoy, it's not always effective in helping you achieve tangible results. For instance, perhaps you have a passion for cooking and want to open a small restaurant. However, opening a restaurant requires a lot of work completely unrelated to cooking. It's easy to use this as an excuse to give up and return to cooking as a hobby unless you have specific reasons why you *must* absolutely open that restaurant.

Similarly, you may love writing, but you *must* have specific reasons why becoming a full-time writer is a must. Otherwise, you'll continue to write as a hobby.

Don't get me wrong. Passion is powerful and will give you an edge, but you'll also need other powerful reasons to help you keep going when times are tough.

Looking for specific reasons to strengthen your ability to persevere is what I call *Why Stacking*.

For instance, one of my passions is studying the human mind to help people reach their full potential. My goal related to that passion is to make a living publishing books to help people become their "best self."

Now, to boost my motivation and ensure I achieve this specific goal, I developed inspiring reasons why my vision *must* become a reality. In the case of self-publishing books on Amazon, the benefits are straightforward and relate to:

- Being my own boss
- Having the freedom to work whenever I want
- Being able to travel whenever I want, and
- Having the ability to increase my revenue.

By *Why Stacking* all these benefits together and combining them with my passion for writing and helping others, I have boosted my motivation and persevered far more than I otherwise would.

You should consider doing the same thing with your passion by stacking as many "whys" as possible. The more compelling reasons you can come up with, the more likely you are to succeed long term. The key is to be specific and to make sure your "whys" speak to you at an emotional level. Let's see what this looks like by using the above examples. Specific reasons why being my own boss appeals to me are:

- It allows me to avoid the rush hour traffic. I can't stand crowded places and can't imagine having to use public transport every working day for forty years.
- I can work from home. At heart, I'm a real introvert and I like working from home. I'm far more productive when I'm by myself in a quiet environment, and that's what I enjoy the most.
- I don't like being told what to do. I've always been far more motivated when I'm doing things on my own rather than when a teacher or a boss issued instructions.
- I'm in charge of my own destiny. I experience a stronger sense of autonomy and control when I work for myself.
- I always have work to do. I will never again be in a position where I have no work but have to stay at the office because the rules force me to.
- I can focus only on what is productive. I don't need to attend unproductive meetings or work on low-value tasks that don't fundamentally improve the business.
- I can have integrity. In one of my previous jobs, I had to cold call companies and lie about who I was and what my intentions were just to obtain information.

Here are some specific reasons why having the freedom to work whenever I want is important to me:

- I can take breaks whenever I fancy.
- I can work as little or as much as I need to.
- I can wake up late or work until late at night if I wish.

And now for a number of specific reasons why being able to travel whenever I want is a must:

- I can visit my family when I choose to do so.
- I can attend interesting workshops or seminars without having to take days off or begging my boss for the leave.
- I can live and work in any country I choose. I love learning languages, and I'm interested in exploring different countries. To be able to do so, working for myself is an absolute must.

And finally, here are some specific reasons why having the possibility to increase my revenue is appealing:

- I am rewarded whenever my revenue increases which is highly motivating.
- If I grow my business, I know I will reap all the financial benefits. On the other hand, if, as an employee, I help my company make a million dollars, I will get little or no reward other than the occasional "thank you," if I'm lucky.

This is just the tip of the iceberg in terms of reasons why my goal of making money from my writing is essential for me. To be honest, when I discovered I could make money online doing what I love, I knew I had to make it happen no matter what obstacles stood in my way. As we'll see in the next section, this level of commitment and determination is a major component of success.

The different levels of "whys"

I believe four main motivators drive our behavior: Pain, pleasure, ego and love. When you are in control of your destiny, you can use these motivators to help you identify your "whys." Here is a brief description of each:

Pain: is what you want to shy away from. Wanting to avoid painful situations will compel you to take action. In the previous examples, pain includes:

- Commuting
- Spending my life doing something I don't enjoy
- Having little or no freedom, and

- Having a boss tell me what to do.

Pleasure: is what you want to gravitate toward, which is basically the opposite of pain. For me, pleasure includes:

- Being able to work from home
- Doing what I love, and
- Having freedom to act and do as I please.

Ego: is the desire to develop or maintain your sense of pride. For instance, it could be making your parents proud, being admired for your work or proving naysayers wrong. For me, it's a healthy dose of each.

Love: is the desire to contribute to something bigger than yourself. You can think of it as being akin to your "life's purpose." This could be a desire to make a difference in the world and to feel good as a result of it. For me, it is receiving emails from people telling me I helped changed their lives in some way.

As it happens, these four motivators are not equal in weight or importance. Whenever possible, I advise you to focus mostly on love and pleasure and use ego and pain whenever you need a short-term motivational boost. For instance, I often relied on ego and pain after a long day of work when I needed a spurt of motivation to work on my online business.

Please note, the more aligned you are with your purpose, the more you will rely on love as your main motivator. Similarly, a good understanding of your core values and personality traits will help you leverage the pleasure motivator more effectively.

* * *

Action step

Why Stacking: Write down all the reasons your goal is an absolute must for you in the **Action Guide** (*Section IV. The Power of Passion - Strengthening Your Whys*).

Bonus tip: whenever you feel your motivation is waning, take a sheet of paper and write down why the goal is important to you. Reignite the passion by reminding yourself why you even set your goal in the first place. Visualize all the wonderful things that will happen when you reach your goal. You might also want to go through your list of whys on a regular basis.

Turning your passion into an "obsession"

Being passionate is not enough. You must develop a healthy obsession or, as Napoleon Hill wrote in *Think and Grow Rich*, a "burning desire" to achieve your goal.

More recently, Angela Duckworth, in her book, *Grit: Why Passion and Resilience are the secret to success*, also stresses the importance of obsession. I believe obsession is a combination of passion and perseverance. When you are really passionate about something, you don't give up easily, do you?

Now you have written down all the reasons you must achieve your goal, you should feel more motivated to do whatever it takes to achieve it. Most people believe passion is something you either have or don't have. While certain people are definitely more passionate than others, I believe we can all strengthen our passion over time. You can actually *choose* to become more "obsessive." As a rule of thumb, the more committed you are to your vision—and the more compelling reasons you have to achieve it—the stronger your passion will grow.

How perseverance can lead to intense passion

Note that the intensity of your passion further grows as you keep persevering in the face of multiple setbacks and disappointments. Each time you refuse to give up you will develop more determination. Whenever you encounter intense setbacks, you will be forced to reconnect with your initial passion and to ask yourself why you even started along the route in the first place. This repeated questioning and continuous search for clarity and meaning will lead you to develop a burning desire.

For this reason, instead of thinking of passion as something you either have or don't have, I encourage you to see it as the natural process you go through as you progress toward your goal. Whenever you face setbacks, use this as an opportunity to strengthen your passion and seek clarity and meaning.

Now you have developed a stronger belief in yourself and in your vision, you've clarified what you want and have defined your passion, you're ready to take the next step. You are ready to **commit**.

PART II

ACTIVATING THE POWER OF COMMITMENT

1

ARE YOU COMMITTED OR ARE YOU MERELY INTERESTED?

> The difference between involvement and commitment is like ham and eggs. The chicken is involved; the pig is committed.
>
> — Martina Navratilova, former professional tennis player.

Most people never really commit to anything. They never make their goals a *must*. Instead, they look for ways out and keep Plan B in the back of their mind. While having a backup plan is smart, to achieve challenging targets that will transform your life, you must be willing to commit wholeheartedly to your goals.

Commitment is the key difference between success and failure and will often determine whether you achieve your wildest dreams or live a mediocre life. When you fail to decide what you want and fail to commit to it, your mind wanders around, jumping from one goal to another, your focus becomes blurred and your confidence wanes.

Conversely, when you commit to achieving a specific goal and eliminate all your excuses, you access the power of your mind. You become more resourceful, your confidence grows, and your focus is where it should be

—on your goal. You progressively remove the uncertainty most people experience by deciding success has to happen no matter what.

Remember, committing is never casual. As Jim Rohn said, "*Casualness leads to casualty.*" The path to achieving the life you need must start with commitment. Great athletes, CEOs and other high performers are not just interested, they are committed to their goals, and you should be, too.

Whenever you find people who fail to achieve their goal, you'll generally find they lack commitment. Human beings have the incredible power to achieve extraordinary feats, but to do so they must be fully committed. In general, people struggle with commitment because:

- They don't truly believe their goal is possible (lack of belief)
- They don't know what they want and therefore feel stuck (lack of clarity), and
- They haven't come up with enough compelling reasons to motivate them to take action (lack of passion).

Look back at a time in your life where you failed to achieve a goal. Be honest with yourself. Were you one hundred percent committed to the goal or were you uncertain, indecisive and unmotivated?

Fortunately, once you know what you want (power of clarity), develop the belief you can do it (power of belief) and create enough compelling reasons for achieving your goal (power of passion), you'll find it relatively easy to commit fully to your goal.

Being committed to your goal means:

- **You're willing to learn whatever you need to learn to get where you want to be.** You never stop learning and are willing to set aside your ego to absorb any information that will help achieve your goal. You don't tolerate excuses like, "I don't know how to do it." Instead, you commit to learning whatever you need to (see *The Law of Humility*).
- **You refuse to give up until you attain the results you want.** You persevere for years and commit to your goals long term. Even better, you write down a specific date a few years in the future

and resolve to keep going until you reach that date. Whenever you feel like giving up, you remind yourself of the set date and refocus on your goal. This will help you focus on your major goal(s) and can prevent you from feeling overwhelmed or discouraged (see also *The Law of Perseverance*).
- **You constantly seek to raise your standards.** You ask yourself how you can improve. You look back at what didn't work and learn from your mistakes.
- **You swallow your pride.** Instead of becoming defensive when people criticize you or tell you to do things differently, ask yourself, "Is there any truth in that?" You accept feedback and, as much as possible, you learn from your mistakes. Again, you're committed to do whatever it takes to achieve your goal.

The bottom line is you *must* be committed. You've never heard of people becoming the best in their field because they showed a mere interest in it. People who design the life they want, do so because they are totally and utterly committed to it.

If you are committed to your goal, you will find a way, otherwise, you'll find an excuse.

* * *

Action step

Complete the exercises in the corresponding section of the **Action Guide** to assess your level of commitment (*Part II. Activating the Power of Commitment*).

PART III

MASTERING THE LAWS OF SUCCESS

1

UNDERSTANDING SUCCESS IS A PROCESS

To be successful, you must understand what success is and how it works. Most people hold misconceptions and often fail to realize what it really takes to succeed.

Success follows a specific process and requires you adopt a different mindset from the norm. While successful people understand that success is a process, most people believe success is an event that can happen almost overnight. They buy into the idea of a magic pill, a lottery win. Unfortunately, they won't lose forty pounds in thirty days by buying a $29.99 course. Neither will they be making $10,000 per month in thirty days with little effort for just $49.99. In short, there is no "magic bullet."

Anything of value—whether it is developing an intimate relationship or building a heart-centered business—takes a great deal of time and effort. This is what makes them so valuable. Needless to say, hard work is one of the prerequisites to success. It may seem common sense but it's worth repeating because most people largely underestimate the amount of work necessary to achieve their goals. In many cases, people give up before the game even starts, taking far less action than necessary to achieve their targets.

Let me give you an example. When I lived in Japan, many people asked me how I learned to speak Japanese so well. Many wished they could speak English as fluently as I speak Japanese. I told them the truth: I worked hard. But it didn't seem to be a convincing answer to these people. They assumed it must have been something else. They assumed I must have been a gifted linguist.

Surprisingly, I've rarely, if ever, seen someone wishing to speak a language—or achieve any other goal—do the required work to achieve the results they say they want. Most people seem to believe that by studying merely fifteen minutes a day for a few months they should be able to speak a language. When they can't, they assume something is wrong with them. I spent over ten thousand hours studying Japanese while living in Japan for almost a decade. Do you call that being a gifted linguist? No, I just followed one fundamental rule for success. I applied consistent effort over a long period of time.

This example clearly illustrates how most people hold unrealistic expectations. They assume success should come quickly and easily, which leads them to take insufficient action and give up prematurely.

Success takes time and effort because, for most endeavors, there is a significant learning curve and limited spots available. For instance, whenever a new business offers promising opportunities, people rush to buy shares in the company, which leads to fierce competition and an increase in the share price. In 2010, you could have made a lot of money publishing crappy e-books on Amazon. In 2018, that's impossible, because more people have entered this market, and Amazon's sales algorithm has become smarter.

Usually, the lower the barrier to entry, the fiercer the competition will be. Self-publishing on Amazon in 2018 is a great example. The barrier to entry is extremely low. If you can create your own cover—which you can do for free—you could technically release a book without spending a dime. However, the poor quality e-book probably won't sell. These days, to be successful as an independent writer, you need to develop a whole set of skills and arm yourself with patience, which is no different from any other businesses or meaningful goal in life. To succeed, you must (among other things):

1. Write quality books that people want to read

2. Create covers that actually sell your books
3. Write book descriptions that actually sell
4. Understand Amazon's sales algorithm (most indie authors earn a majority of their income from selling books on Amazon)
5. Market your books effectively, which can be done in multiple ways (Amazon ads, Facebooks ads, posting on social media, etc.), each method having its own learning curve
6. Develop relationships with authors in your niche, and
7. Brand yourself so that you stand out from the crowd, etc.

To sum up, you need to develop a deeper understanding of how success works and go through several years of hard work before you can achieve your goal, whether the goal be personal or professional.

Now, let's dive into *The Seventeen Laws of Success*. Each law, when applied individually, will increase the odds for success. As you combine them and practice them consistently, you'll dramatically increase your chances of success long term.

2

THE LAW OF HUMILITY

> Pride is pleasure arising from a man's thinking too highly of himself.
>
> — BARUCH SPINOZA, PHILOSOPHER.

The Law of Humility states that, by swallowing your pride and accepting the requirement to change everything needed to achieve your goals, you will dramatically increase your chances of success.

Swallowing your pride

Have you ever watched the show called *The Profit*?

In this fascinating show, serial entrepreneur, Marcus Lemonis helps struggling businesses, by offering his own money in exchange for an equity share of their businesses.

What surprised me the most in the show was how defensive many business owners were. Their behavior and attitude seemed to be the main reason they were struggling. They were:

- Unwilling to reconsider the way they do business and let go of things that clearly didn't work
- Unwilling to take responsibility for their poor results. Instead, they blamed employees, customers, suppliers or external circumstances
- Unable to let go of control and allow employees do their job, and
- Unable to empower employees and nurture an environment in which they could grow.

I encourage you to watch the show. You'll find a few episodes on YouTube.

Here is another example of the role pride plays in someone's success. The internet marketing guru, Dan Lok, once complained to his mentor about his lack of success. Despite having started many different businesses, he was always struggling.

"*I'm not making enough money, I'm struggling. I don't know why. My customers, they are like, cheap. They are really difficult to deal with. Oh man I don't know. The economy kind of sucks. And I think I'm paying too much taxes.*"

His mentor asked him to stop and said, "*It is very simple Dan. Let me teach you something. If your business sucks, it's because, as a business person,* you *suck.*"

Ouch!

One of the major reasons people fail to achieve their business goals (and other goals), is they are unwilling to look in the mirror and accept the need to change everything that doesn't help them achieve the results they want.

For instance, many authors say they want to sell more books, but:

- They cling to their original cover ideas because the cover looks beautiful, even though the cover doesn't sell
- They are unwilling to lower the price of their books or offer temporary discounts because they spent so much time writing their book, and
- They shy away from promoting their books, believing that if they write a great book, readers will come by some form of thought osmosis.

I take authors as an example but the same goes for any profession. Your ability to swallow your pride and take responsibility for where you are now will largely determine your chances of success. Being humble enough to realize you may be wrong and accepting you don't know everything is a critical component of success.

In the end, the key question is whether you're getting results. Results don't lie. Ask yourself:

1. Is your business generating revenue?
2. Are you making money from your side business?
3. Did you win the competition?
4. Have you lost weight?
5. Are you happy?

To succeed long term, you must be willing to look at the harsh truth and make changes when necessary. You must be radically honest with yourself and take responsibility, even when you're only partially responsible.

Perhaps you believe you excel at what you do while reality shows a different picture. Or you may think your business idea is amazing, but it only works on paper. If so, you need to take a step back and ask yourself whether you are *really* doing what it takes to achieve success. If you keep doing what you've done today, this week or this month, will you achieve that specific goal? If the answer is no, you're going to have to change something!

Remember, the more you take responsibility for your life, the more likely you are to succeed. For instance, you can't improve your intimate relationship if you believe you're right and your partner is wrong. My gut tells me Dan Lok's mentor would say the following, "*If your intimate relationship sucks, it's because you suck as a partner.*"

You must let go of pride and accept one hundred percent responsibility for your life. Only then, can you make the changes you need to create the life you want.

Fighting complacency

Complacency is a major reason people fail to achieve their goals in the long term. It generally results from the belief you don't need to improve anymore because you're already doing a good enough job. While there is great value in celebrating your wins, you also run the risk of slackening off.

Remember, since success is a process and not an event, you must embody the process every day. Resting on your laurels is the antithesis of what success is. You can't expect to have a fulfilling marriage if you stop putting in the effort after getting married. Neither can you expect to have a thriving business that remains prosperous for decades if you're not working on it consistently. Yet, this is what many people tend to do.

To maintain success long term, you must try to improve each and every day, continuously. To learn more about the importance of continuous improvement, refer to *The Law of Mastery* and *The Law of Continuous Learning*.

In your field, you can always learn something new to help you perform at a higher level and make a bigger contribution. If you feel you already know enough, you're probably overconfident. And it might be time to humble yourself and become obsessed with improving your skills.

To achieve the result you want in any area of your life, swallow your pride, stop being complacent and change *everything* you need to change to be where you want to be in the future.

* * *

Action step

Write at least one reason pride could stand in your way. Answering the following questions in the **Action Guide** might help you (*Part III. Section I. The Law of Humility*):

- How can pride prevent me from achieving the results I want in life?
- Do I refuse to ask for help?
- Am I unwilling to change things that don't work?

3

THE LAW OF MASTERY

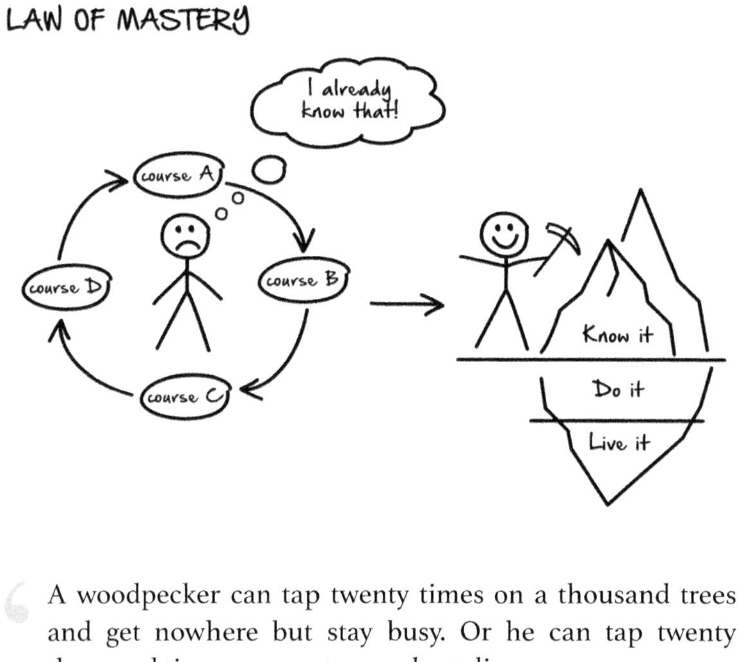

> A woodpecker can tap twenty times on a thousand trees and get nowhere but stay busy. Or he can tap twenty thousand times on one tree and get dinner.
>
> — SETH GODIN, THE DIP.

The Law of Mastery states that if you apply anything you learn and delve as deep as you can, you will inevitably generate positive results over the long term.

Developing a mastery mentality

To reach your goals, it is essential you develop a "mastery mentality," which means the ability to master any area you choose to focus on. Most people just scratch the surface of any given subject. These people adopt a short-term mentality, trying to achieve results as quickly as possible. They fail to go deep enough with their new ventures and keep jumping from one opportunity to another. They don't take their relationships to a new level because they're afraid of showing vulnerability. Or they give up learning a new skill after repeated failure.

If you look at one area of your life in which you're struggling, you'll probably notice that you failed to adopt a mastery mentality. The key characteristics of the mastery mentality are:

1. Focusing on one thing at a time
2. Practicing what you know intellectually, and
3. Repeating the process until you reach a high level of skill.

For instance, let's say you've tried to create an online business for the past three years. You may have tried to shoot video on YouTube, sell products on Amazon, do affiliate marketing, or publish Kindle books. Now, you may wonder whether any of these things really work.

However, the real question is, do other people have real success with these businesses? If so, how come you don't?

Often the problem isn't whether something works, but whether you will *make* it work. Will you learn to master the process, so you can achieve the results you want, or will you dabble and barely scratching the surface of the new challenge?

* * *

Action step

Complete the following exercises using your **Action Guide**:

1. On a scale of 1 to 10 (1 being false, 10 being true), evaluate yourself on the following points:

- I easily avoid jumping from one opportunity to another.
- I put into practice everything I read or learn about.
- When I'm learning something new, I keep practicing until I reach a high level of mastery (*Part III. Section II. The Law of Mastery - Developing a Mastery Mindset*).

2. Look at one area of your life in which you aren't satisfied. How much of what you know have you actually put into practice? Have you mastered the fundamentals in this area?

1. Focusing on one thing at a time

Have you ever jumped from one training course to another or tried several diets without seeing positive results? If so, you're a victim of the so-called "Shiny Object Syndrome." This syndrome stems from the false idea that success is an event, not a process, and thus should come easily and quickly if you can only find the "right method" for you. In reality, as we've already seen, anything of value takes *a great deal of time* and *a great deal of effort* and must involve a specific process.

I've seen high achievers trying to do multiple things at the same time. Unfortunately, I've seldom witnessed people succeeding in doing so. Most of the time, these individuals work hard just to get mediocre results at best. The truth is, you don't need to be a genius to achieve great results, but you need to focus on one thing (or a very few things) and go as deep as you can with it until you master it. Only then should you consider moving on to the next thing.

Remember, perseverance is key.

Below are some examples of what focusing on one training course or program at a time actually means:

- Choosing the best diet and sticking to it long-term until you actually lose weight
- Focusing on one or two skills needed to further your career and becoming proficient at these skills, and
- Promoting your business only on one or two social media platforms until you achieve tangible results.

This is not to say you can't succeed in multiple areas of your life, create several businesses or learn dozens of new skills, because you definitely can. But, it's far more effective to do so by mastering one new skill at a time.

Although you might have hundreds of items on your to-do list, I encourage you to select a couple of things you're really excited about and focus on these for the next few months. Once you have made demonstrable and consistent progress, you can focus on other things on your to-learn list. This approach is usually less overwhelming and, I promise you, far more effective over the long term than trying to do everything at once.

To give you a personal example, at one point I was doing all the following activities:

- Shooting YouTube videos
- Creating video courses
- Doing "Facebook Lives"
- Posting daily on Facebook
- Blogging
- Guest posting, and
- Writing books.

I was working hard but not seeing much progress. One day, I decided to eliminate the things that failed to produce satisfying results such as the YouTube videos, "Facebook Lives" and the guest posts. Instead, I focused almost entirely on three things:

- Writing more books
- Marketing using PPC ads, and

- Connecting with other authors in my genre.

Suddenly, my whole business process felt less overwhelming.

What about you? If you were to focus on only two specific actions, which ones would be most likely to pay off?

For more on the importance of focus, refer to *The Law of Focus.*

* * *

Action step

Look at all the projects and goals you're working on right now. Select the one you're the most excited about and write it down using your **Action Guide**. Turn it into a SMART goal and spend most of your effort on it over the next few weeks or months until you obtain the results you want (*Part III. Section II. The Law of Mastery - Focusing on One Thing at a Time*).

2. Practicing what you know intellectually

Because you think you "know" something intellectually, it doesn't mean you actually know it. This is a dangerous assumption that prevents many people from achieving the results they want. "Knowing" a topic is almost useless without experience. For instance:

"Knowing" everything about nutrition doesn't help unless you eat more healthily.

"Knowing" the entire content of this book is useless unless you actually apply the knowledge.

"Knowing" how to approach a man or a woman with a view to building a relationship is irrelevant if you don't actually make the approach.

Many people know the theory but fail to take action. This is the main reason they fail to make changes in their lives. Simple yet true. They're the ones who "already know that," and for whom "there is nothing new." When it comes to achieving any goal, however, what matters is the ability to execute. Intellectual knowledge is of little help if action isn't taken. If I had merely read self-help books without applying what I'd learned, my life wouldn't have changed much.

* * *

Action step

Write down all the things you know at an intellectual level but haven't truly mastered **in your Action Guide**. That is, things you've read or heard about but haven't really applied in your life (*Part III. Section II. The Law of Mastery - Practicing what you know intellectually*).

3. Repeating the process until you reach a high level of mastery

True knowledge requires repetition. Every master of every craft is a master of repetition, be it a martial arts expert, a successful writer or an accomplished comedian. Anything not practiced consistently and fully integrated at the subconscious level remains purely intellectual. You can't learn to drive a car by reading books. You must practice over and over until you internalize all the different skills and moves required to be a good driver. Nor can you become a public speaker without actually practicing speeches in front of an audience over and over again.

Don't dismiss the power of *The Law of Mastery*. This law, when applied consistently, will massively improve your long-term success rate.

Coach and online entrepreneur, Stefan Pylarinos, breaks down mastery into three levels: *knowing*, *doing* and *living*. *Knowing* is when you only know something intellectually but have little or no experience doing it. *Doing* is when you're actually performing the skill or task. *Living* is when you've become a living example of it.

Below is a concrete example:

- Knowing level: reading a book on nutrition.
- Doing level: Changing your diet to eat more healthily.
- Living level: Eating healthily every day as an ingrained way of life.

Go deep with whatever you need to learn to achieve your goal. Find a great training course or program and apply everything consistently until it becomes second nature. Keep doing this and return to the fundamentals when you struggle, and you'll achieve far better results long term. Also, remember, the mastery mentality is a way of thinking. Once you understand it (by living it), you'll be able to use it for all sorts of goals.

* * *

Action step

Answer the following question in your **Action Guide**:

If you were to master one thing to make the biggest impact in your life, what would it be? (*Part III. Section II. The Law of Mastery - Developing a Mastery Mindset*).

4

THE LAW OF FOCUS

> I focus on one thing and one thing only—that's trying to win as many championships as I can.
>
> — Kobe Bryant, professional basketball player.

The Law of Focus states that intense focus on the most important area of your life right now will yield great results while positively impacting most of the other areas of your life.

If you're like most people, you want an exciting career, a good paycheck, a healthy body and plenty of time to spend with your family.

However, the reality of the day-to-day living seldom provides us with such a harmonious life. To make major changes in your life, I encourage you to let go of the idea of "balanced life." Instead, realize that you must often accept living an unbalanced life in the short term to design your ideal life in the long term.

The same way you can't build four successful businesses at the same time, you can't transform all the areas of your life at once. You must take a more focused approach.

I believe there are five major areas in life:

- Career
- Finance
- Health
- Personal growth, and
- Relationships

With a balanced approach to life, you would spend roughly twenty percent of your time and/or effort on each of these areas. Now, what kind of results do you think you would get under these conditions? Ask yourself if you could be successful with all the following goals:

- Build your ideal career (career)
- Get your finances right (finance)
- Lose weight (health)
- Change yourself (personal growth), and
- Find your soul mates (relationships)

If you're doing well in each of these areas, it may work temporarily. But if you're like most people, you'll probably find it difficult to achieve the results you want in all the areas simultaneously.

What if you're overweight, single, broke and hate your job?

Do you think spending only twenty percent of your time and effort on each of these challenges will allow you to overcome them?

A better strategy would be to focus a majority of your effort—eighty percent or more—on one major area. For instance:

- If you're currently overweight and at risk of becoming severely ill, you should probably focus most of your effort on improving your diet, losing weight and, as a result, improve your overall health.
- If you hate your job and wake up depressed every day, you should probably focus on changing your career.
- If you've been single for a long time and feel lonely, perhaps starting a relationship or making new friends should be your immediate priority.
- If you're broke and can't afford to buy healthy food or go on a date, you should probably gear most of your efforts toward improving your financial situation.

Success and balance don't work well together. It is unlikely you'll be able to design the life of your dreams without a certain level of obsession. This is because success tends to like intense focus sustained over an extended period.

After you make satisfying progress in one specific area, you can move on to replicate the same process for other areas of your life.

You can change your life faster than you think

We grossly overestimate what we can do in six months, but largely underestimate how drastically we can improve our lives in five or ten years. In five years, you can change one or two key areas of your life. In ten years, you can transform most or all of them. That's why it's so critical to adopt a long-term mentality and learn to remain consistent over the years (see also *The Law of Long-Term Thinking*).

As you learn to focus most of your efforts on one major part of your life, you'll start seeing noticeable changes not only in that area, but also in other areas, too.

For instance, when you find a job you love, you'll probably experience less stress which may lead you to feel better. As a result, you might have more motivation to make changes in other areas of your life.

My point is, every area of your life is interdependent, and changing one will often change the others.

Give yourself enough time, stay focused and remain consistent while being kind to yourself, and you'll be amazed at what you can accomplish in a few short years.

* * *

Action step

Answer the following question in your **Action Guide**: Among the five areas—health, finance, relationships, career, personal growth—if you were to focus most of your effort right now on only one, which would most help transform your life? (*Part III. Section III. The Law of Focus*).

5

THE LAW OF EFFECTIVE ACTION

> Efficiency is doing things right; effectiveness is doing the right things.
>
> — PETER DRUCKER, MANAGEMENT CONSULTANT AND AUTHOR.

The Law of Effective Action states that success becomes almost inevitable when you identify key actions and focus on them daily.

Sometimes, we work hard but fail to realize that what we do is highly ineffective. On my website, I used to have banners redirecting visitors to my books' sales pages on Amazon, hoping they would generate sales. But did you know the average click-through rate for this type of banners is a pitiful 0.03%?

This means only three out of 1,000 people who visit my website will click on the ad banner. Even worse, among this three, on average only four percent will buy the book. Assuming my blog generates 10,000 unique visitors this month, the banners will generate a mere 1.2 sales. This demonstrates that relying on banners is the perfect example of an ineffective action.

Identifying the process

It doesn't matter how badly you want to land your dream job, lose weight or become wealthy. Unless you put in place a specific and successful process, you won't achieve your goal. The process is what you do every day to reach that goal. It entails answering "yes" to the following question:

"If I keep doing what I'm doing today, will I achieve my goal?"

The better you can identify the most effective process to get from point A, where you are now, to point B, where you want to be, the higher your chances of reaching your goal.

To design the optimal process, you must identify the best strategy possible. It isn't nearly as complicated as it sounds, though. Some people have already achieved the same goals you are targeting. Thus, all you need to do is to identify these people and reverse-engineer what they did. There is no need to reinvent the wheel. For instance, as Brendon Burchard explains in his book *High Performance Habits,* he discovered that to become a number one best-selling author, he would likely have to focus on the following tasks:

- Finish writing a good book (sounds obvious).
- Find an agent (for a major publishing deal) or self-publish.
- Build an email list of subscribers (using social media and blogging).
- Create a book promotion page and offer great bonuses to encourage people to buy the book, and
- Get five to ten people with a big email list to promote the book.

These are the five core tasks he chose to focus most of his time on to publish a number one best-seller (which he did).

Similarly, you'll notice there are usually a few strategic moves—generally between three and five—that will allow you to achieve your goal with the minimum effort and the maximum impact. Make sure you spend time identifying these moves. Doing so will save you a great deal of time and effort down the line.

Here are some tips to help you discover your strategic moves:

Identify role models who have achieved the results you desire and observe what they're doing. What actions do they take every day? What are their core beliefs?

Interview people who have achieved your goal and ask them what they would do if they were in your position. You will be surprised how many successful people will be willing to help. Consider asking them the following questions:

- What do I need to do to be in your position? What skills do I need to develop? What mindset do I need to adopt?
- What is the secret to your success?
- What is your daily routine? What key tasks do you perform every day?
- Knowing what you know now, what would you do to go from where I am today to where you are now as quickly as possible?

Brainstorm strategic moves. Write down all the things you could do to achieve your goal. Come up with a list of at least twenty things. Now, ask yourself:

- If I could do only one task every day to achieve my goal, what would it be? If I could do a second task what would it be? Repeat the process until you have your three to five core tasks.

Hire a coach. A coach might be expensive, but they can allow you to reduce your learning curve and save you months or even years of struggle (among other benefits).

* * *

Action step

Using the tips above and your **Action Guide**, write down what you could do to identify the strategic moves you need to adopt to achieve your goal (*Part III. Section IV. The Law of Effective Action*).

Using the 80/20 Rule

The 80/20 rule states that twenty percent of your actions will yield eighty percent of your results. Regardless of your goal, there are always a few things that will produce greater results than all the other things combined. Make sure you identify these key tasks and focus most of your time on them.

The 80/20 rule works in many situations and can help you achieve all sorts of goals with significantly less effort. Here are some examples:

- Want more fulfilling relationships? A few friends bring you eighty percent of your happiness. Spend more time with them.
- Want to make more money? About twenty percent of your clients bring you eighty percent of your revenue. Identify these high value clients and find a way to serve them better and therefore sell them more products.
- Stressed by your current job? Identify the twenty percent of the tasks that are generating eighty percent of your stress and see if you can delegate them, do fewer of them or approach them in a different way.

Note that the accurate ratio might not necessarily be 80/20. It could be 90/10 or 70/30, but the principle is the same.

* * *

Action step

Complete the following exercise in your **Action Guide** to help you identify the few things that really move the needle up the success slope (*Part III. Section IV. The Law of Effective Action*).

1. What three to five strategic moves do you need to focus on to achieve your biggest goal?

2. Select one of the areas below and apply the 80/20 rule:

- **Relationships:** Who are the few people who bring the most of your joy? How could you spend more time with them?
- **Happiness:** What few things do you derive most of your happiness from? What could you do to make them your main points of focus?
- **Work:** What few tasks really move the needle toward success? How can you make them your priority?
- **Thoughts:** What few thoughts generate most of your joy and excitement? What practice will allow you to focus on these thoughts more often?
- **Worries:** What few worrying things generate most of the stress in your life? How can you eliminate these worries from your life?

6

THE LAW OF DELIBERATE PRACTICE

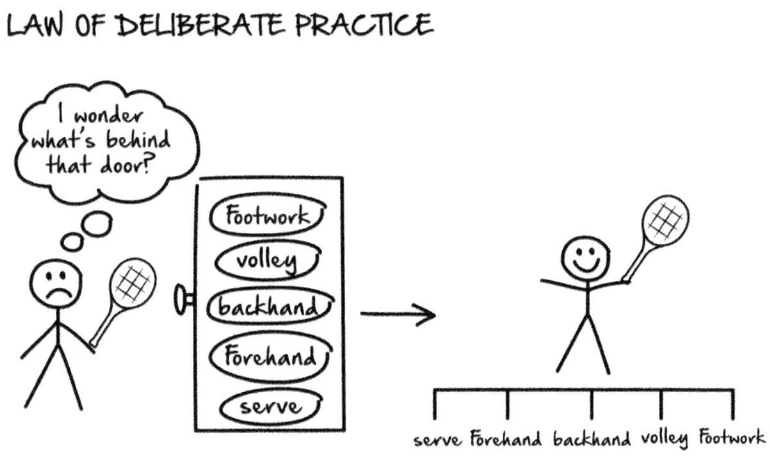

> Practice does not make perfect. Only perfect practice makes perfect.
>
> — Vince Lombardi, American football coach.

The Law of Deliberate Practice states that you'll become far more competent at what you do if you design effective practices aligned with your goals.

Why do some people consistently make progress while others stay at the same level of competence for years? The former individuals practice with a specific aim in mind while the latter keep doing the same thing without an effective practice in place.

According to researchers at Harvard Medical School, doctors with decades of experience don't seem to provide better patient care than those with just a few years of experience. You would expect a doctor with decades of experience to be significantly more skilled than one who's just getting started, but that doesn't appear to be the case. It also applies to nurses, and I suspect, the same goes for many other professions.

In short, the main reason most people are stuck at a certain level of expertise is not that they lack intelligence or talent, but that they fail to make the necessary efforts to improve their performance.

What exactly is "deliberate practice"?

In their book *Peak, Secrets from The New Science of Expertise*, Anders Ericsson and Robert Pool state that deliberate practice:

- Builds skills for which effective training techniques have already been established.
- Takes place outside of people's comfort zone, requires significant effort and is generally not enjoyable.
- Involves specific, well-defined goals.
- Requires a person's full attention and conscious actions
- Entails regular feedback
- Both creates and relies on effective mental representation, and
- Almost always involves working on existing skills or building new ones by focusing specifically on some aspect of those skills that need to be improved.

As you can see, deliberate practice is quite different from the way most of us practice our craft. In fact, I would suggest that most people have never applied deliberate practice before.

The famous novelist, Stephen King, wrote, "*If you want to be a writer, you must do two things above all others: read a lot and write a lot.*" He has a good point but what if it's more complex than that?

Benjamin Franklin felt he needed to do more than merely read and write a lot. He focused on improving three specific skills: his writing style, his vocabulary and his sense of organization. In a nutshell, here is Benjamin Franklin's schedule for deliberate practice:

- **Writing style:** He made notes on articles from *Spectator*, a high-quality newspaper, which he would use to rewrite the articles a few days later. He would then compare his version with the original article and modify it accordingly.
- **Vocabulary:** He rewrote *Spectator* essays in verse and then in prose, to compare his vocabulary with the original article.
- **Organization:** He wrote summaries of every sentence in a particular article on separate sheets of paper. He would then wait a few weeks before challenging himself to write the article in the correct order and compare his work to the original.

How you can apply "deliberate practice"

To help explain *The Law of Deliberate Practice,* I'll use tennis to demonstrate how practicing deliberately differs from playing casually. To do this, we'll review each characteristic of deliberate practice.

Deliberate Practice builds skills for which effective training techniques have already been established.

Chances are the goal you are trying to reach has already been achieved by someone else. As we've seen when we discussed *The Law of Effective Action*, there is no need to reinvent the wheel.

If you wish to become a professional tennis player, why not copy the practices used by people who have already reached that status? This might entail hiring a coach, reading sports magazines or watching training videos on YouTube.

The same goes for any other area in which you want to improve your skills. Whether you want to create a business, become a musician or enhance the quality of your relationships, you will find people who have already achieved these goals. They will be able to show you the way.

In an interview, Arnold Schwarzenegger recalls how one day he saw the whole blueprint for becoming a bodybuilder in an article featuring Reg Park, a bodybuilder, actor and three times Mr. Universe. He used the same blueprint to start his training. Could it be that simple?

Sometimes however, the path toward your goal is unclear. Perhaps there isn't any proven method to achieve your goal. If so, do some research and try your best to design your own blueprint. You can always refine it over time.

Deliberate practice takes place outside your comfort zone, requires significant effort and is generally not enjoyable.

If you keep doing the things you already know how to do, your progress will slow, and you'll eventually reach a plateau, being unable to improve your performance.

Playing tennis with your friends every Sunday might be fun, but how much progress can you reasonably make? On the other hand, practicing your serve for two hours is tedious, but when done right, will turn you into a better player.

Deliberate practice involves specific, well-defined goals.

Working on your first serve is a specific and well-defined goal. Playing with your friends on Sundays isn't, since you probably won't be working on a specific skill, you'll just be having fun.

To give another example, merely rehearsing a speech will be less effective in the long term than focusing on a specific skill, such as voice projection, body language or rhythm.

Deliberate practice requires an individual's full attention and conscious actions.

If you practice serves with focus you will improve. However, if you go through the motion mechanically—as you would when washing the dishes—your progress will be slower and you'll reach a plateau very quickly.

Deliberate practice entails regular feedback.

For instance, as you practice your first serve, you receive instant feedback on the results. In addition, if you work with a coach, they will point out what you need to focus on in order to improve. As you make adjustments based on that feedback you will almost inevitably improve.

Deliberate practice both creates and relies on effective mental representation.

Deliberate practice and repetition creates a mental representation of patterns of information held in long-term memory. These patterns contain various elements—facts, images, rules, muscle memories or relationships—organized in a coherent way. Deliberate practice leads to the creation of effective mental representations which, in turn, enhance performances. For instance, mental representation allows taxi drivers to find their routes in complex cities and enables chess masters to play blindfolded.

A tennis player who has practiced the same move repeatedly will have a far more effective mental representation of the action than someone who plays tennis as a hobby.

Deliberate practice almost always involves working on existing skills or building new ones by focusing on a specific aspect of those skills.

When you play tennis with your friends on Sunday, you're generally not trying to improve any particular skill. You may improve your game slightly over time, but your progress is likely to be slow and rather random.

On the other hand, when you apply deliberate practice, you break down a skill or a craft into different components. Tennis can be seen as one skill that encompasses a whole set of other skills. Some of those skills are first serve, second serve, forehand, backhand, volley, footwork and so on. If we further break down these macro skills, sub-skills might involve isolating a muscle via a well-defined exercise to improve a certain shot or practicing a specific exercise to increase your stamina.

Therefore, if you want to improve, identify a few key sub-skills and work on them deliberately and consistently until you see some improvement.

* * *

Action step

Look at one particular goal you would like to accomplish in the near future. What skills do you need to develop to achieve that goal? And what specific exercises do you need to perform/practice to make progress as quickly as possible? Go through each characteristic of deliberate practice as identified by Anders Ericsson and Robert Pool, and write down your answer in your **Action Guide** (*Part III. Section V. The Law of Deliberate Practice*).

7

THE LAW OF CONSISTENCY

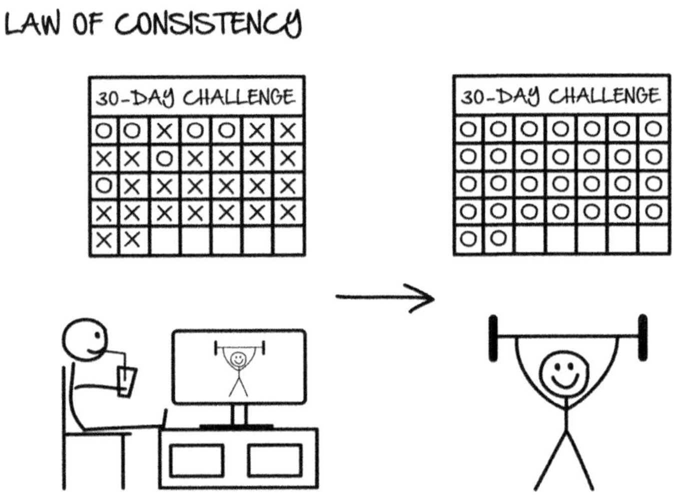

> It's not what we do once in a while that shapes our lives. It's what we do consistently.
>
> — Tony Robbins, motivational speaker.

The Law of Consistency states that simple daily habits repeated for a few years lead to exceptional results.

Success is a process that requires both repetition and regularity. To increase your chances of success long term you must learn to develop consistency. Here are some examples of consistency:

- The Olympic swimmer, Michael Phelps, only missed five days of swimming in a seven-year training program.
- The famous writer, Stephen King, writes every day, including his birthday and during Christmas. He aims to write six pages a day.
- Russian author, Leo Tolstoy, wrote every day, saying: "*I must write each day without fail, not so much for the success of the work, as in order not to get out of my routine.*"

Consistency is one of the best predictors of success because, in the end, your ability to do something consistently whether you feel like it or not will determine whether or not you achieve your goals. There will be days when you don't want to do the work, but if you can force yourself to work anyway, your chances of success will increase significantly.

Consistency is more important than intensity

People largely underestimate the power of consistency while they overestimate the power of intensity. They tend to believe they can change in a matter of days or weeks just by working hard. Who is more likely to obtain the best results long term—the person who commits to running two minutes every day for a year, or the person who goes to the gym four times a week for two hours and gives up after a month?

Becoming a high performer doesn't require you do great things; it requires you do small things *consistently* every day to the best of your ability. These small things build over time and, as you keep transferring new habits to your subconscious mind, you will become far more effective. If you are a regular driver, think back to the first time you drove a car. I bet it felt overwhelming and a little scary. Today, after practice and years of experience, the act of driving has become effortless.

Remember, consistency is more powerful than intensity. Starting small not only reduces the risk of procrastination, but it also boosts your self-esteem and helps you generate momentum (see *The Law of Momentum*).

Adopting daily habits

By now, you should have identified your three to five key moves. If not, return to the section, *The Law of Effective Action*.

Now, look at your strategic moves. How could you turn them into daily practices? If you were to perform certain moves every day, which ones would allow you to make the most progress toward your goal?

For instance, if you're an aspiring writer, you could block a specific amount of time every day to write or decide on a number of words to crank out daily. Also, you could connect with other authors in the same genre by emailing one new author each day. Marketing would probably be another strategic move. Jack Canfield, author of the popular series, *Chicken Soup for The Soul*, did five things every day for over a year to promote his book. Perhaps, you could do something similar.

The bottom line is that identifying your strategic moves and turning them into consistent daily habits is one of the most important things you can do to promote success.

How to become more consistent

One of the most effective ways to develop consistency is to implement a morning ritual. Morning rituals have been popularized by Hal Elrod in his book, *The Miracle Morning*.

A morning ritual can serve two main purposes. First, it can help prime your mind by deciding how you want to feel. For instance, this can be done by performing gratitude exercises, by listening to music or by using visualization and affirmations. Second, it can allow you to work consistently on key tasks by making them part of your morning ritual. For instance, when I was an employee, I would spend thirty to forty-five minutes writing before going to work.

A crash course in creating a morning ritual

You can create your own customized morning ritual to help you condition your mind and get rid of limiting beliefs. In my book, *Wake Up Call*, I present nine steps to help create a morning ritual that will support you in achieving your goals. They are:

1. **Clarifying your "why".** Make sure you have a clear objective in mind when you create your morning ritual. You might want to experience particular emotions, or you might want to focus on a specific goal, using affirmations or visualization.
2. **Getting excited about your morning ritual.** Drink your favorite coffee, read your favorite book, or spend time with your family. Do whatever excites you.
3. **Identifying obstacles and preparing yourself mentally.** Look for potential hurdles you may encounter as you create your morning ritual. If you failed to implement a morning ritual in the past, ask yourself why.
4. **Selecting the components of your morning ritual.** For a more balanced morning ritual, select activities that will feed your body, mind and soul. Try exercise, meditation, journaling and things of that nature.
5. **Deciding how much time you have available.** It could be as little as ten minutes or as much as an hour, but be consistent.
6. **Removing roadblocks and distractions.** Prepare everything you need the night before. Go through your morning ritual first thing in the morning to avoid procrastination.
7. **Setting yourself up for success.** Make sure you get enough sleep. If necessary, create an evening ritual as well. Whenever possible, go to bed at the same time every night. You can also set your intentions the night before and visualize the tasks you want to work on the next day.
8. **Committing one hundred percent.** Commit to your morning ritual. Don't be casual about it.
9. **Undertaking the Thirty-Day Challenge.** To strengthen your commitment, dedicate at least thirty days to your morning ritual.

If you want to learn more about how to create an exciting morning ritual, check out my book, *Wake Up Call: How to Take Control of Your Morning and Transform Your Life*.

* * *

Action step

Complete the exercises below using the **Action Guide** (*Part III. Section VI. The Law of Consistency*).

1. Look at the three to five strategic moves you've identified previously. Now, what could you do to turn them into daily habits?

2. Select the one move you could do first thing in the morning to help you achieve your main goals. Stick to it for at least thirty days.

8

THE LAW OF IDENTIFICATION

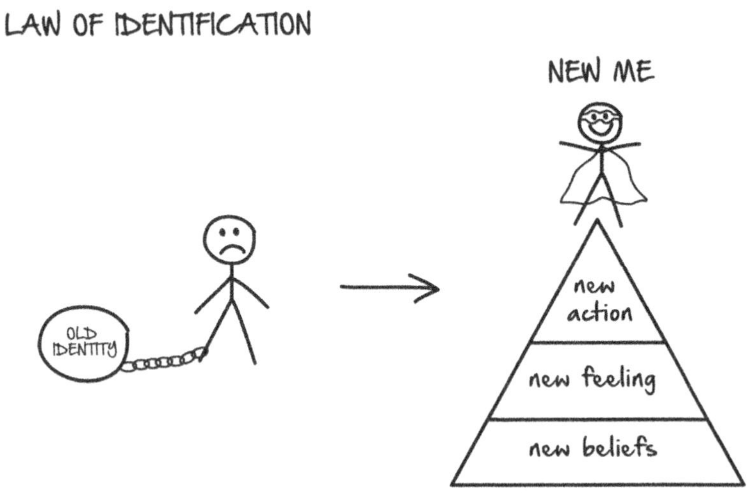

> Your main job in life is to create the mental equivalent within yourself of what you want to realize and enjoy in your outer world.
>
> — Emmet Fox, author.

The Law of Identification states that the more you think, feel and act like the person you wish to become, the faster you'll achieve your goals.

What a goal really is

Have you ever wondered why some people achieve their goals while others fail? Is it because they work harder? Well, hard work can't be the only answer, otherwise, all hard-working people would reach their goals. To answer this question let's consider the following example:

Imagine you are currently fifty pounds overweight and have been struggling to lose weight for years. Now, put yourself in the shoes of someone with the "ideal weight" such as a personal trainer. Imagine you —as a personal trainer—wake up one day carrying an extra fifty pounds of unwanted weight. How would you react?

I'm betting you would be shocked. You would think, "This is not who I am. This is unacceptable," and you would instantly start transforming your body. You would remove all junk food from your house and exercise daily until you returned to your ideal weight. And you would do it as quickly as possible. It would still be hard, but you would do it regardless. This is inevitable.

Why is it inevitable? It's because you have a specific image of what your body *should* look like and a specific idea of your health. This image is so closely linked to your identity you would inevitably return to your original weight. The only unknown is how long it would take.

Money is another good example. There are many stories of multi-millionaires who lose all their money and make it back, seemingly in a heartbeat. Why is that? It's because they have a multi-millionaire identity. They perceive money in a different way from the rest of us and, while $20,000 feels like a lot of money for most people, for them it's no big deal. As a result, they are comfortable negotiating huge deals or borrowing large sums of money. The difference in mindset goes far beyond their perception of money, however. Their relationship with failure, the way they interact with people and how they think is also different from the majority of the population. It is no wonder that even when bankrupt, they behave differently from other people in the same financial situation. This is inevitable.

This example leads to the following question:

What if reaching your goal isn't so much about going from point A to point B, but more about shifting from Identity A, who you are, to Identity B, who you need to become to achieve your goal?

I believe both approaches are interconnected. By taking the necessary actions to move from point A to point B, you become a new person. And by shifting your identity and focusing your effort on becoming a different person, you support the actions needed to move to point B.

Shifting your identity

Think of one of your goals. What shift in identity would need to happen for you to achieve this particular goal? How different would you be as a person?

The first step to shifting your identity is to think of what the personal development blogger, Steve Pavlina, called the "side effects" of having achieved your goal. Or, to put it another way, what would be different about your life once you've achieved your goal? Ask yourself:

- What would be your core beliefs about yourself and about the world?
- How would you think differently?
- How would you feel?
- What would you do differently?
- What new habits would you have developed?
- What old habits would you have rejected?

If you're unsure of the side-effects of your career goal, talk to someone who has achieved your goal and ask them the following questions:

- What do I need to believe to be in your position?
- What habits would I need to develop?

To achieve your goal, your beliefs and actions must match those of people who have achieved this goal. Now, it won't happen overnight. The key is to start closing the gap by progressively shifting your identity over time.

For instance, let's say my goal is to be a successful non-fiction writer. What would be the side-effects?

- I would write every single day as do most successful writers.
- I would introduce myself as a writer without feeling embarrassed.
- I would contact other successful writers like me.
- I would expect to sell a lot of books.
- I would find it normal to be invited to speak at events or even on TV or radio.
- I would expect to be paid a lot of money to speak at events.

* * *

Action step

Write down the side effects of having already achieved your goal using the **Action Guide** (*Part III. Section III. The Law of Identification*).

9

THE LAW OF CONDITIONING

> A human being always acts and feels and performs in accordance with what he imagines to be true about himself and his environment.
>
> — Maxwell Maltz, author of Psycho-Cybernetics.

The Law of Conditioning states that you can train yourself to experience any emotion if you focus on feeling that particular emotion for long enough.

You have the power to recondition your mind to experience more positive emotions. In many regards, your mind works like an app which you can program to do whatever you want it to do. The major problem is that many people, instead of doing the programming themselves, let other people or their environment do it for them. They feed their mind with negative news and disempowering beliefs. This daily exposure to negativity generates toxic thoughts that become their default position. Not surprisingly, these people experience far more negative emotions than they otherwise would.

Here is the truth: if you don't program your mind, someone else will. Therefore, it is your responsibility to take control of your thoughts and choose the information you feed your mind every day.

The best way to condition your mind is to adopt powerful daily rituals. One example would be to create a morning ritual (see *The Law of Consistency*). Another way to do this is to set specific intents as you move from one segment of your day to another. When performed consistently, these small rituals will, in the long term, have far more impact than you might imagine.

Successful people adopt daily rituals to condition their mind and perform at their best. Here are some ways you can condition your mind:

- Adopting a gratitude practice every morning.
- Having the intent to be fully present when you greet your spouse after returning from work.
- Focusing on three things you're proud of before going to bed.

Remember, the more often you feel a certain emotion, the easier it will be for your brain to reproduce it.

The bottom line is that through conscious repetition and clear intent, you can train your mind to generate positive emotions. Make sure you use *The Law of Conditioning* to help you achieve your goals.

* * *

Action step

Select one daily habit that will help you condition your mind to experience more positive emotions in your life. If you can, make it part of your morning ritual by combining it with the thing you committed to doing in the **Action Guide** section, *The Law of Consistency* (*Part III. Section VIII. The Law of Conditioning*).

10

THE LAW OF ATTRACTION

> The key to success is to focus our conscious mind on things we desire, not things we fear.
>
> — Brian Tracy, author and motivational speaker.

The Law of Attraction states that the more you focus on something, the more likely you are to attract that thing into your life.

You may have heard of *The Law of Attraction* before, but in this section, we'll introduce a simple and straightforward version of it.

1. Focusing on what you want

To activate *The Law of Attraction*, you must constantly focus on what you want. Many people say they want to make more money, be happier or have better relationships, but they never make it their focal point. I believe you *cannot* fail to make progress long term if you keep focusing on what you want. Define exactly what you want and make it your main focus. Remember, clarity is power.

Here is what success expert, Brian Tracy, wrote is his book *Goals!*

"*Many thousands of successful people have been asked what they think about most of the time. The most common answer given by successful people is that they think about what they want—and how to get it—most of the time.*"

Note, you must focus on what you want, *not* on what you don't want. It may seem like there isn't much of a difference, but the difference is significant. When you focus on what you don't want, your focus is on the negative things you want to prevent from happening. And we've already learned that whatever you focus on, you tend to attract. It also generates negative emotions and puts you in a disempowering state of mind.

Look at the examples below and see which options are the more empowering:

- Ruminating on your lack of money.
- Or thinking about all the positive aspects of making more money in the near future.

- Reading news about the poor shape of the economy.
- Or reading books written by wealthy people with an "abundance mindset."

Remember, whatever you choose to focus on consistently, you will eventually attract in the long term. Money is just one of many examples. Thus, make it a habit to think of what you want as often as possible and commit to making it a reality (see *Power of Commitment*).

Please note, you can condition your mind to experience positive emotions by implementing daily habits such as consuming motivational materials or eliciting feelings of gratitude through various exercises.

2. Appreciating what you already have

There are a myriad of things for which you should be grateful, such as your overall health, your ability to walk, talk, hear, feel and taste or having access to the countless services available in the Information Age. Learning to experience a deep sense of gratitude for all the things you already have is a powerful activator of *The Law of Attraction*. Conversely, failing to count your blessings generates feelings of scarcity and prevents you from unlocking the resourcefulness and optimism required to improve your life.

We'll discuss in more detail how to cultivate gratitude in the section *The Law of Gratitude.*

3. Activating the power of your subconscious mind

Your subconscious mind is the most powerful mechanism on earth. To achieve the success you want in life, you must leverage its power on a regular basis. One of the reasons *The Law of Attraction* can be so effective is precisely because it allows you to use the power of your subconscious mind to a greater extent than most people manage.

Here are a few key characteristics of your subconscious mind:

It records far more information than the conscious mind

Your subconscious takes in far more information than your conscious mind ever could. It is also in charge of regulating bodily functions. Imagine how exhausting it would be if you had to consciously remind yourself to grow your hair, make your heart beat or regulate your body temperature. Fortunately, the subconscious takes care of all these things for you.

Have you ever experienced buying a new car and then seeing the same make and model everywhere as you drive around?

It's not because there are more cars of that same type now than before. It's just that you didn't notice them before. But your subconscious mind did. Now, take a moment to complete the following exercise:

1. Look for any red item in your room for about five to ten seconds.
2. Now, close your eyes.
3. Try to remember any blue item in the room.

You probably had a hard time coming up with even one blue item. This shows that whatever you're looking for, your subconscious mind will help you find it by processing information available in your environment. This is another reason to clarify what you want. By doing so, you tell your subconscious mind what it should be looking for.

The subconscious cannot discern what is true from what is false

Your subconscious mind isn't judgmental and has no ability to assess whether something is true or not. It will inevitably accept what you have been told repeatedly. In fact, by age seven, you will have already built your own model of reality from beliefs you've accepted as true.

More interestingly, your subconscious mind cannot tell the difference between your imagination and what actually happens, which is why athletes, chess players and musicians use visualization to improve their skills.

For instance, in the 1960s, an experiment was conducted to evaluate students on their ability to make free throws in basketball under various conditions. Students were divided into three groups. The first group was asked to train twenty minutes a day for twenty days, a second was asked not to train at all and the third was asked to imagine themselves making free throws twenty minutes a day for twenty days. Ultimately, the group of students who practiced only in their imagination performed almost as well as those who practiced in reality. Specifically, those who practiced in reality improved their scores by twenty-four percent, while those who practiced in their imaginations improved by twenty-three percent. Students who refrained from both visualization and physical training showed no improvement. This experiment has been replicated many times since and has continued to produce similar results.

The bottom line is that your subconscious mind will accept anything as true provided you repeat it enough times and/or emotionalize your vision correctly.

The same process is used to indoctrinate religious extremists. Once people have been told the same thing a million times, they lose their ability to even question the validity of a so-called fact. Because they're convinced their beliefs are facts, no one can question those beliefs without triggering their inbuilt defense mechanism.

Here's another example. Imagine your parents have been telling you that you will never amount to anything. How likely are you to achieve great things in your life? Now, the statement, "you'll never amount to anything" is *not* a fact, it is an opinion. The fact is, human beings can always grow and improve, and we can certainly outgrow these limiting beliefs.

The subconscious is more powerful than your conscious mind

Whenever there is a conflict between your subconscious mind and your conscious mind, the former always wins. This is because your conscious mind is just the tip of the iceberg, while your subconscious mind is the submerged part that drives most of your thoughts and behaviors.

By turning your attention to what you want as often as possible using visualization, you will reprogram your subconscious mind (i.e., you will modify the invisible force that drives most of your thoughts and behaviors). As you do so, you will shift your beliefs and generate new thoughts. These thoughts will drive new behaviors and allow you to obtain better results.

As you focus consistently on what you want, you cannot fail to change your life in the long term. So, whether you want more money, deeper fulfillment or better relationships, keep thinking about those things and never cease to clarify exactly what they mean to you. Meanwhile, consume materials that expose you to the new mindset you want to adopt.

* * *

Action step

Complete the following exercise using the **Action Guide** (*Part III. Section XI. The Law of Attraction*).

- Spend as much time as possible focusing on the main area you wish to make a change in (see *The Law of Focus)*. Throughout your day, keep thinking of the ideal results you want to achieve in that specific area.
- Adopt a gratitude practice each morning (see *The Law of Gratitude*).

11

THE LAW OF RESET

> Create your future from your future, not your past.
>
> — Werner Erhard, author.

The Law of Reset states that every day is a new day, completely independent of the previous one.

If you have been carrying the weight of the past on your shoulders, how would you feel if you could reset your life and start afresh today? Wouldn't this make you feel lighter? Well, it is entirely possible. In fact, it's inevitable if you choose to live in the present rather than in the past.

While many of us become stuck in the past, the truth is our *present* determines our future not our past. Nothing prevents you making different decisions today compared with the ones you made yesterday and, by doing so, you will create a different—and better—future. Every day you receive a credit of 86,400 seconds. It's up to you to seize this new opportunity to become the person you want to become and to design the life you want to live.

Bear in mind, if you don't do what's necessary to move toward your vision today, you probably won't do it tomorrow either. Studies show that we tend to perceive our future self as having more discipline and being better in many ways than our current self. However, the truth is your future self will *not* change unless your present self makes the change.

What you do *today*, not what you've done in the past or what you think you'll do in the future, will allow you to live the life you want, and I can't emphasize this enough.

Making different decisions

We are largely creatures of habit. We have our own routines and tend to feel, think and act the same way every day. Because we've been doing the same things for so long, we tend to be blind to all the possibilities and opportunities in front of us, which makes us feel stuck. In short, we lack an overall perspective.

Life, however, is like a chess game, each moment offering an opportunity to make different decisions when faced with an almost infinite number of possibilities. In truth, we only feel stuck because we start our day with the same beliefs and ways of thinking we had yesterday and the day before. However, as we change the way we think and act, new opportunities cannot fail to arise.

Consider the following: on average we make 35,000 decisions each day. Now, how many of these decisions do you think you need to change to start altering your whole existence? Remember, just a couple of habits repeated consistently every day will yield huge results.

In effect, your past is almost irrelevant and does not have to determine your future. Your future is the result of what you do today, not what you have done in the past, and not what you say you'll do tomorrow.

* * *

Action step

Complete at least one of the following exercises using the **Action Guide** (*Part III. Section X. The Law of Reset*).

1. **Brainstorming exercise:** Write down everything you could do differently. Could you do something different upon waking up? Adopt at least one new positive habit in your life? Contact someone you haven't contacted for a while? Start journaling?
2. **7-Day Challenge:** For the next seven days, begin your day as though you have been born again, and feel the field of possibilities ahead of you.
3. **Visualization exercise:** Forget about everything—who you think you are, your past, your future et cetera—and reconnect with the present moment. Close your eyes to do this exercise. Now, spend a couple of minutes envisioning your future and the life you wish to create.

12

THE LAW OF INTENT

> Everything that I do is with a purpose and intent of wanting to make a difference.
>
> — Katrina Adams, professional tennis player.

The Law of Intent states that the more purposeful you are during your day, the better results you will achieve.

Developing the habit of "setting intent" will radically transform your life. Before starting a new activity simply ask yourself, "What's my intent here?"

Imagine if you were to ask yourself that question on a regular basis, how much more deliberate would your actions be? How much more would get done?

Setting the intent before a new activity is what Brendon Burchard refers to as "managing transitions." This means you make a conscious effort to separate your day into different segments. For instance, you may have had a bad day at work, but it doesn't mean your bad mood has to spill over into your home life. Setting a clear intent before a new segment of your day is an effective way to live a more deliberate life. This will allow you to achieve better results in every area of your life.

Setting intent in your daily life

Look at your current life. How much intent is there behind the things you do every day?

Do you choose how you want to feel and think before going to work? Do you consciously choose to switch your energy and mood once your working day is over?

Imagine if you decide to set clear intents every day. How much will your life change over the coming months?

Identify key transitions

We can see our day as a succession of segments and choose to move from one to the next with a clear intent. Some key daily segments are:

- Waking up
- Eating breakfast
- Leaving home
- Arriving at work

- Eating lunch
- Going home after work
- Eating dinner, and
- Going to bed.

While most people go through their day largely without a conscious plan (without intent), you have the power to decide how you want to feel during any part of the day.

- You can wake in the morning excited to start your day and with a deep sense of gratitude.
- You can eat breakfast intending to be fully present and available to your spouse and your kids.
- You can arrive at work with a clear intent to be as productive as possible and focus on the things that matter.
- You can eat lunch with the intent of releasing all the tension developed from work and decide to relax fully.

As you choose your intent for specific segments of each day, and consistently and consciously choose how you want to feel, after a few weeks, these feelings will become natural, and everything will start to happen almost automatically.

So, what about you? What are the key transitions in your daily life? Start asking yourself the following questions:

- What do I want my intent to be here and now?
- What am I trying to do here?
- How do I want to present myself in this segment of my day? Excited? Confident? Loving? Determined?

* * *

Action step

Think of your typical day. Use the **Action Guide** to decide: which one segment of your day could you bring a specific intent to, that will have the most positive impact? For the next seven days, resolve to set your desired intent before moving to that specific segment of your day (*Part III. Section XI. The Law of Reset*).

13

THE LAW OF CONTINUOUS LEARNING

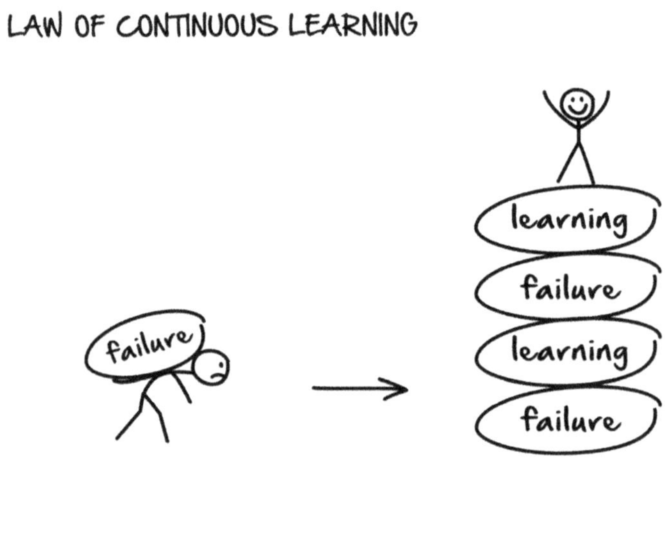

> If you leave your growth to randomness, you'll always live in the land of mediocrity.
>
> — Brendon Burchard, high performance coach and motivational speaker.

The Law of Continuous Learning states that getting better is inevitable if you keep acquiring new skills and learning from failures.

Developing the habit of continuous learning

It is your responsibility to educate yourself continuously after you graduate school and land your first job. See yourself as the CEO of your own life. Take responsibility for learning everything you need to learn to achieve your goals. Remember, nobody cares as much about you as you do yourself. Don't delegate the role of educating yourself to your company or society.

The sad truth is, many people stop educating themselves once they leave school. According to a 2018 survey conducted by the Pew Research Center, twenty-four percent of Americans say they haven't read a book in the past year. Many people will seldom or never read a book after they graduate. Don't be like them. Instead, continuously seek new knowledge until the day you die. Continuous learning allows you to improve and increase the value you can provide to your company, your family and friends, and society as a whole. The more you educate yourself, the more doors will open for you.

Nowadays, with the internet, you have access to a vast amount of information, and you can use it to learn anything you want. You have no excuse not to educate yourself.

The Law of Continuous Learning also states that the more you struggle in life, the more you must make learning a priority. As the motivational speaker, Jim Rohn, said, "*Miss a meal if you have to, but don't miss a book.*" You cannot afford not to learn. The long-term consequences are too severe.

Failure and success—same things?

Have you ever considered that failure and success may actually be the same thing? As a result of the way failure is perceived in most societies, we tend to see failure as the opposite of success. However, that's total rubbish. The only true failure is when you refuse to learn lessons from your so-called failures.

- Is an entrepreneur who failed in multiple businesses before creating a multimillion-dollar business a failure?
- Is someone who went on hundreds of dates and suffered hundreds of rejections before finding the love of their life a failure?
- Is a writer who received hundreds of rejections before winning a major publishing deal and becoming a best-selling author a failure?

Again, success is a process. You don't succeed by avoiding failure, in fact, *you fail your way to success*! Failure is thus part of the success process, not separate from it. Continuous learning involves regular "failures" before your ultimate and inevitable success.

I've witnessed countless people being held back by their fear of failure and, as a result, they don't live the life they want. I don't want that to happen to you. Here is how I encourage you to see failure:

As a feedback mechanism and part of the process called "success."

Airplanes are a great example of how this feedback process works. An airplane will drift off track during most of the flight. Without constant intervention and adjustment, either by the pilot or his buddy, the auto-pilot, the airplane would never reach its destination. The tiny adjustments made during the journey ensure the plane reaches its final destination rather than landing hundreds of miles away. "Failures" work the same way. They serve as feedback by letting you know when you need to make adjustments to reach your final destination.

Your ability to learn from your mistakes and make adjustments as you proceed is key to achieving your goals.

The bottom line is, by continuously educating yourself and learning from your mistakes, you maximize your chances of success (see also *The Power of Reframing*).

* * *

Action step

Commit to learning. Use the **Action Guide** and dedicate at least ten minutes every day to reading educational material that will help you achieve your long-term vision (*Part III. Section XII. The Law of Continuous Learning*).

14

THE LAW OF PERSEVERANCE

> I had the happy privilege of analyzing both Mr. Edison and Mr. Ford ... so I speak from actual knowledge when I say that I found no quality save persistence in either of them, that even remotely suggested the major source of their stupendous achievements.
>
> — Napoleon Hill, author of Think and Grow Rich.

The Law of Perseverance states that you can and will achieve far more than you can ever begin to imagine if you keep persevering and refuse to give up prematurely.

Perseverance is one of your most undervalued assets. Use it to your advantage and learn to stick to your goals *until you attain the results you want*. When most people reach the stage when they would give up, you must keep going. When you decided to pursue your goals you probably didn't think, "I'll just give it a try and give up like everybody else as soon as the going gets tough," did you? No! You were committed to achieving your goal. So, keep this in mind while you progress toward your goal.

The 90% rule

This rule states that around 90% of people will give up too soon to ever be in competition with you.

To illustrate this rule, let's return to our previous example of Kindle Publishing. Let's say out of 10,000 people who want to make a living writing and publishing books on Amazon, only ten will succeed (quite close to actuality I would suggest). It sounds incredibly competitive, doesn't it? Among these 10,000 people, how many are actually committed to doing what it takes to succeed? What percentage of them will still be writing and publishing after three years? A rough estimate is that ninety percent of them will see writing as a hobby and won't make it full time.

Among the 1,000 people left, ninety percent will have disappeared within twelve to twenty-four months and won't be willing to do what it takes to succeed. This leaves only one hundred people.

Among these one hundred people, between half and two-thirds will not succeed because of their inability or unwillingness to learn from their mistakes. For example, they probably won't do what's necessary to sell more books such as temporarily lowering their prices or learning to do effective marketing (see *The Law of Humility*).

We are now left with only thirty to fifty people. Among these burgeoning authors, the ones who adopt the principles described in this book are much more likely to succeed. Because these individuals think long term and understand it takes time to get results, they will persevere and overcome challenges and disappointments along the way. They will improve continuously and put into practice everything they learn. As a result, they will achieve results long term even in such a hugely competitive market.

Of course, these are rough estimates. The aim here is to help you understand the role that perseverance plays in success.

The relationship between luck and perseverance

As I've already stated, success is a process, not an event. You don't become successful because you get lucky (except on some rare occasions such as winning the lottery). While luck can certainly play a role in someone's success, luck (both good and bad) tends to average out over the long run. You may be out of luck for a few months or even a few years, but if you stay focused on your goals and follow the process laid out in this book, you are likely to "get lucky." The key is to remain consistent over the long term, work hard and never give up. Obvious, right?

The truth is, the more action you take, the more likely you are to find something that works. If you take five times more action than the average Joe and keep focusing on your goal for three years while he gives up after four months, which of you is more likely to succeed?

In my personal and professional life, I've seen that perseverance often pays. For instance, I noticed that in one of my previous jobs, if I "cold called" enough people and for long enough, I would generally end up talking to the right people. As you learn to persevere, in many situations you'll be able to figure out ways to achieve your goal.

It might also help to think of perseverance as part of the natural process of selection. If one hundred people want the same thing, why should you be the one getting it? Why not see each obstacle as a test designed to assess your degree of motivation? Temporary setbacks, discouragement and self-doubt are part of life's selection process.

The relationship between commitment and perseverance

A commitment is a declaration to yourself and to others that you will reach your goals and stick to your promises. When you commit, you activate your perseverance muscles and make it far more likely you'll reach your goals. In short, commitment puts you in the top five percent of people who will not give up prematurely. For more see *Part II. Activating the Power of Commitment.*

To strengthen your perseverance muscles, you must regularly:

- Recommit to your goal
- Reignite your passion and the whys behind your goal
- Strengthen your beliefs, and
- Seek clarity regarding what you want.

You may have noticed that your ability to persevere happens naturally as you leverage the three fundamental powers of success (belief, clarity and passion) and (re)commit to your goal.

How to persevere more than anybody else

Imagine how much more you would accomplish if you could persevere ten times more than you currently do. Perseverance is a skill, and it can be learned. In addition to leveraging belief, clarity and passion, you can also use various tools and exercises to help you persevere.

In **Part IV** of this book, we'll discuss in great detail what you can do to skyrocket your ability to persevere. For now, let's have a look at what I called the *Bullet-Proof Timeframe*. This part is an extract from my book, *The One Goal: Master the Art of Goal Setting, Win Your Inner Battles and Achieve Exceptional Results.*

In, *The One Goal,* I discuss how to win your inner battles and develop an exceptional mindset to achieve your wildest goals and dreams in great detail.

The Bullet-Proof Timeframe

The *Bullet-Proof Timeframe* reminds you that you *do* have time. It also encourages you to keep working on your goal until you reach a specific point. This specific point is generally a deadline set two to three years from now.

The *Bullet-Proof Timeframe* provides the following benefits:

- It forces you to select a goal that truly matters to you. Why would you care about some distant deadline two to three years from today if the goal is unimportant?
- It reminds you that you have time. As you step back and consider the big picture, you're able to maintain a long-term perspective. This, of course, enables you to persevere.
- It helps you avoid "Shiny Object Syndrome," and prevents you from jumping from one thing to the next because you feel you aren't getting results fast enough. This is a major trap many people fall into.
- It gives you the option of giving up. You can give yourself total permission to give up, but *only* once you've reached a specific deadline, and never before.

You may wonder how long the *Bullet-Proof Timeframe* should last. For a major goal, I recommend a two to three year timeline, which is long enough for you to see tangible results. Please note, it's very common for people to give up within a year, and this is precisely the mistake I want you to avoid.

The art of persevering smartly

While perseverance is extremely important, it is even more essential you learn to persevere the correct way, or you may end up wasting your time.

In her book, *Grit: Why Passion and Resilience are the Secrets to Success,* Angela Duckworth tells the story of the cartoonist, Bob Mankoff, whose cartoons were rejected over two thousand times by the *New Yorker* between 1974 and 1977. One of his cartoons was eventually accepted and he ended up becoming a contract cartoonist for the prestigious newspaper.

The interesting part of Mankoff's story is that he didn't just persevere randomly; he had a strategy. First, he studied old cartoons published by the newspaper to discover what they had in common. As he recalls, "*I went to the New York Public Library and I looked up all the cartoons back to 1925 that had ever been printed in the New Yorker.*" He realized they all had one thing in common—they made the reader think. He also noticed every cartoonist had their personal style. Believing he could do as well as the other cartoonists, he continued submitting cartoons until one of them finally was accepted.

Here are three key lessons we can learn from Bob Mankoff's story:

1. **Passion leads to perseverance.** Bob Mankoff thought of himself as a funny guy and was willing to do what it took to make a living from his passion.
2. **We must do our best to understand what works.** For business-related goals, what works is often what people want. Once you understand what your clients or customers want, you can offer them the right products or services. In Mankoff's case, it was what the *New Yorker* (and its readers) wanted. Perhaps he had to compromise a little, but I'm sure he didn't regret doing so (see also *The Law of Flexibility*).
3. **We must have a degree of faith in our eventual success.** This means we must believe that, with enough work and perseverance, we have a reasonable chance of achieving our goals. In this case, Bob Mankoff believed that he could make people think while maintaining his own personal style.

The bottom line is that persevering mindlessly isn't enough to achieve the results you want. You must assess your chances of success long term based on your level of passion, your strengths and your talents, and you must also be willing to change your approach whenever necessary.

* * *

Action step

Implement a *Bullet-Proof Timeframe* for your goal using the **Action Guide**. Commit to not giving up until you reach your specific deadline (*Part III. Section XIII. The Law of Perseverance*).

15

THE LAW OF COURAGE

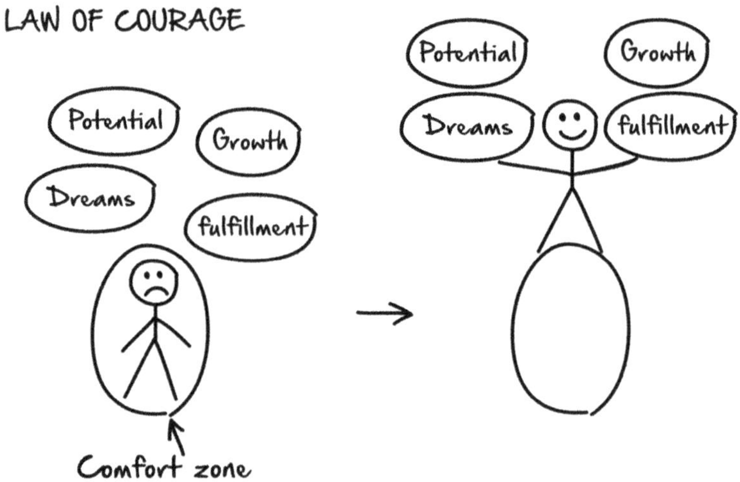

Man cannot discover new oceans unless he has the courage to lose sight of the shore.

— Andre Gide, novelist.

The Law of Courage states that the more often you can face your fear and move beyond your comfort zone, the more you'll achieve in life.

I believe one of the main purposes of life is to overcome our fear and to act more and more from a place of love. All the limitations we impose on ourselves are, for the most part, illusory. Our barriers are mostly mental ones.

Each of us holds a different set of beliefs, some are empowering, others are disempowering. These beliefs determine what we can and cannot do in this world. Some people are so afraid of public speaking they will do anything to avoid having to stand in front of a crowd. Some have so little confidence in themselves they believe they'll never amount to anything and others are terrified of trying anything new.

Have you ever done something you were scared of and felt wonderful afterward? Whenever you overcome limiting beliefs and fears, you often feel an immense sense of pride and joy. It's as though you rediscover your true self. For a brief moment, you see how much more you're capable of doing and feel wonderful as a result.

I believe our inner self wants to expand and rediscover its true nature. Inside us, there is a constant tension between our small self, who wants security and comfort, and our bigger self, who seeks to expand and experience more of what life has to offer.

How much more could you experience if you were able to move beyond your comfort zone and face your fears on a regular basis? How much better would you feel about yourself? And how much more of a positive impact could you have on the lives of other people?

In truth, no human being has ever been able to explore the whole immensity of their potential. We have almost infinite room to grow. We are the only species on earth that, through the power of imagination, can alter the course of its destiny. But to become more, we must develop courage. We must move beyond our comfort zone, even if this means starting something new and scary and facing our fears one at a time.

As we accept the need to feel discomfort, our comfort zone will naturally expand. What we believed was impossible yesterday will become perfectly normal today, and what we fear today will become easy to do tomorrow. When this happens, we will wonder why we've been so easily swayed by imaginary fears.

Such is the fate of human beings, or so it seems.

You have the courage within you to overcome all your limitations. Remember, courage is not the absence of fear. By definition, someone without fear can't be courageous. Courage is recognizing the fear, accepting it is part of the process and overcoming that fear with action. As you move inexorably toward your goals, your ability to face discomfort will not only determine the speed at which you will make progress, but also the likelihood you'll achieve your goal.

Developing courage

In his classic book, *The Magic of Thinking Big*, David J. Schwartz presents a simple formula to overcome fear which can be summed up in three words, "action cures fears."

As this concept suggests, immediate action destroys fear at its roots before it spreads and invades our minds.

Years ago, I went bungee jumping with a couple of friends. We were about to jump from a sixty-seven-meter-high bridge above a river and, when my turn came, I knew that I had to jump right away. If I had hesitated and looked down at the river, fear would have kicked in and I would probably never had jumped. So, when they told me to go, I jumped immediately.

The same happens in our daily life. When we hesitate, we give fear the opportunity to invade our minds. Immediate action is what prevents our minds from generating endless rationalizations and inflated stories that aren't grounded in reality.

A key point to understand is that our brain's primary function is to ensure our survival. This survival instinct tends to prevent us from doing anything new or scary and is our brain's way to avoid wasting energy and enhance our odds of survival. Our brains use rationalization and fear to prevent us from doing anything it perceives as a threat. Even in today's world, where most of us rarely face real physical threats to our survival, our mind interprets things like the risk of rejection and the exposure to new experiences as potential dangers, making us more and more risk averse.

Starting small

Moving out of your comfort zone doesn't mean doing something that scares you to death. You can gradually ease out of your comfort zone by taking small steps. For instance, I'm an introvert and I'm rather uncomfortable putting myself out there. This morning—as I'm writing this book—I was interviewed on a podcast. A few years ago, this sort of thing would have terrified me but, this time, I found it no big deal (though it was still a little uncomfortable). This is because I've already pushed myself beyond my comfort zone in the past by recording YouTube videos. The more videos I recorded, the more I grew used to the process. My next uncomfortable thing was doing Facebook Live. Again, the more experience I gained, the less scary it became. If I hadn't done these things before, being interviewed would have been far more uncomfortable.

The bottom line is, whatever your comfort zone is right now, you can dramatically expand it way beyond your imagination. In a few years from now, you could very well be doing things you would have thought out of the question today. This is a real possibility. Remember, the walls defining your comfort zone are purely created by your imagination.

Doing the impossible

What is the single most impossible thing for you to do? Is it making a speech in front of a large audience? Leading a team? Asking for a promotion? Cold calling a prospect?

Whatever it may be, let me tell you this: it is absolutely possible for you to overcome this fear!

So, what if you could do the impossible? What if you accomplish something today, this week or this month, you had always thought was impossible (for you)? How would it make you feel?

Doing something way beyond your current level of comfort can dramatically expand your comfort zone, and it can do so in a short period of time. Suddenly, you will realize how much more you're capable of achieving. You may even start thinking, "What else can I do?"

This will create a whole new dynamic in your life.

Getting support

Sometimes, finding the courage to take action on your own can be challenging and doing the impossible might be a little too overwhelming (for now).

Years after my bungee jumping experience, I went skydiving. This time it was different. I didn't have to make the jump alone. The expert I was tethered to did. Having someone to help me jump made things significantly easier. The point I'm making is, sometimes you need support to help you move beyond your comfort zone and unlock your potential.

Other people can help you grow by:

Being a role model. Comfort zones vary from one person to another. When you surround yourself with people whose comfort zone is larger than yours, you will start perceiving your fears and limitations differently. For instance, you'll be more likely to overcome your shyness if you share a house with outgoing people. This is because they are likely to put you in uncomfortable situations you normally avoid. Additionally, as you watch them interact with other people confidently, you'll start shifting your perspective into believing you can do the same thing. If you're willing to overcome your shyness, such an environment will help you tremendously.

Holding you accountable. It's easier to take actions and do things that scare you when someone such as a coach holds you accountable. Having an accountability partner can also be effective, providing both of you are fully committed and willing to call each other out (in a gentle and supportive way).

Encouraging you to take action. People can also offer encouragement.

Support from family and friends can be extremely powerful. As we'll discuss in more depth in the section, *Leveraging the Power of Proximity*, your environment is key to your success.

* * *

Action step

What one thing have you wanted to do for a while but put off due to fear? Could you challenge yourself and do it this week? Write down one thing you could do to move beyond your comfort zone in your **Action Guide** (*Part III. Section XIV. The Law of Courage*).

16

THE LAW OF FLEXIBILITY

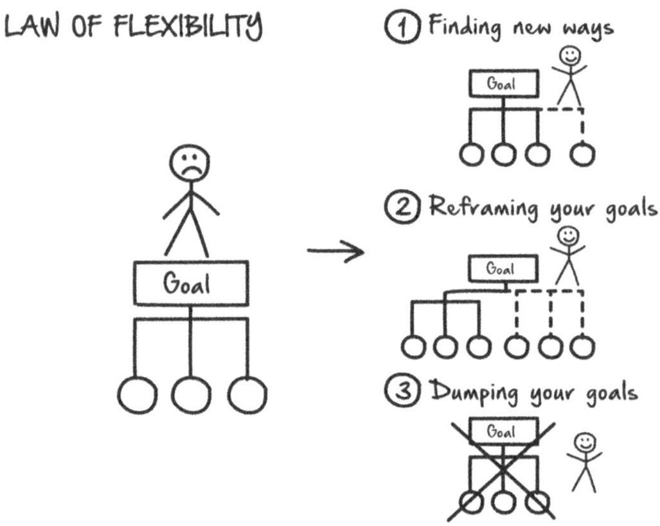

> For a flexible person, it is impossible not to reach his destination, because by using his ability to be flexible, he can easily define a nearer new destination!
>
> — Mehmet Murat ildan, author.

The Law of Flexibility states that the more you are willing to consider all the options available to achieve your goal, the more likely you are to succeed.

1. Finding additional ways to achieve your goal

We often have an idea of what our success should look like, but things don't always go as planned. Sometimes, what we thought would work doesn't and we feel stuck.

A goal is generally divided into milestones you need to pass before you can reach your final destination. However, not all these milestones are necessary. It is possible to find many alternative ways to reach your goals.

Let's take the example of someone who wants to become a writer. Perhaps that person identified "finding a publisher" as a key milestone to achieve their goals and can't seem to reach that milestone. Now, what if reaching that milestone isn't essential in the first place? What if that person could self-publish and make money that way? That's what some writers decide to do when they fail to land a publishing deal. Alternatively, what if that same individual doesn't want to get involved with book marketing, cover design, editing, et cetera? Perhaps they would be better off freelancing or ghostwriting.

Just because one door closes, doesn't mean you have to give up. Remember, if you're committed to your goal, you'll find a way to reach it, otherwise you'll find an excuse. Your greatest skill is your resourcefulness, so don't give up just because your original plan didn't work out as expected. Try an alternative approach. Be committed. Be fluid.

2. Reframing your goal

You may be narrowing your options unnecessarily by believing your current goal is the only one that can lead to your desired outcome. Don't get me wrong, I still believe one hundred percent in the power of perseverance and clarity. If you know exactly what you want, I encourage you to persevere along that path.

However, sometimes your goal might be only one of many manifestations of a bigger purpose. This is why I recommend you spend time identifying your overall purpose. You can then use this as a compass and set your goals with both determination *and* flexibility, knowing you're generally heading in the right direction.

As an example, my purpose is to inspire people to be the best person they can possibly be. Books are merely the medium I use to fulfill my mission, as it is aligned with my introverted personality as well as my talents and strengths. However, if I ever found myself facing a roadblock or if I chose to expand my reach, I might have to fulfill my purpose in a different way. For example, I could do more coaching, hold seminars, create training courses or teach in some way. One thing I will *not* do, though, is give up.

I would like you to think of ways you could reframe your goal to give yourself more flexibility.

To learn how to identify your life purpose and set the right goals, refer to my books *The Passion Manifesto: Escape the Rat Race, Uncover Your Passion, and Design a Career and Life You Love,* and *Goal Setting: The Ultimate Guide to Achieving Goals that Truly Excite You.*

3. Giving up on your goals

Another way to leverage *The Law of Flexibility*, is to give up on your goals. While I recommend you persevere, sometimes it is actually important to allow yourself to give up.

The truth is, you evolve over time. Goals you were originally excited about may not excite you anymore. If so, you must not be afraid to drop them. However, before you give up on a specific goal, I encourage you to ask yourself the following question:

Do I want to give up because I'm scared, lack confidence or feel tired? Or is it because I genuinely don't want to pursue that goal anymore?

Finally, remember that a goal is here to make your life better. While it may be challenging, it should also be exciting and enjoyable most of the time. If not, it might be time for you to dump your goal and work toward a more meaningful one.

We'll talk about the importance of emotional flexibility at greater length in **PART IV. Building Emotional Resilience.**

* * *

Action step

How can you use *The Law of Flexibility* to increase your chances of achieving your long-term goals? Write your answers in the **Action Guide** (*Part III. Section XV. The Law of Flexibility*).

17

THE LAW OF PATIENCE

> Patience is bitter, but its fruit is sweet.
>
> — JEAN JACQUES ROUSSEAU, PHILOSOPHER, WRITER AND COMPOSER.

The Law of Patience states that you must trust the process and remain consistent until you see the fruits of your labor.

As you remain consistent over the long term, you will often reach a tipping point that skyrockets your results, sometimes almost overnight. This is where the myth of the so-called overnight success comes from. While many people think in linear terms, success is far from being linear. In most cases, it is exponential. For instance, it is possible for you to have a sudden breakthrough that dramatically shifts your mindset and generates astonishing results. But, much more likely, thanks to your consistent work, you may finally knock at the right door and find the person or opportunity needed to accelerate your success.

The following story by the motivational speaker, Les Brown, illustrates the power of patience extremely well:

"*The Chinese Bamboo tree takes five years to grow, and when they go through a process of growing it, they have to water and fertilize the ground where it is every day, and it doesn't break through the ground until the fifth year, but once it breaks through the ground within five weeks it grows ninety feet tall. The question is: does it grow ninety feet in five weeks or five years. The answer is obvious.*"

There will always be a gap between the time you plant the seed (i.e., start taking action toward your goal), and the time you witness results. While, initially, you may make good progress, often things slow down at some point. Then, the ambitious goal you set at the beginning of your journey will seem like a pipe dream and you seem miles away from attaining it within the original timeframe. This is when many people give up. It is, however, a normal process most people go through during their journey. I advise you to bear this in mind and remain patient.

Since I started blogging and writing books back in 2014-2015, I've failed to achieve my goals again and again. I keep missing my financial goals, my blog traffic barely increased and my books weren't selling well. Many times I said to myself, "What's the point writing books and articles? Nobody is reading them anyway. Why even bother?"

Despite my repeated "failures," I kept focusing on the process—the work I do daily—rather than focusing on my mediocre results. I remained patient, kept writing books and learned as much as I could about self-publishing. I started analyzing what other writers in my field were doing, trying to pinpoint key activities that may lead to better results. In short, I focused my efforts on improving the process, because I realized it was the only thing I had control over. I trusted the process, believing that, eventually, I would achieve my goal. And you know what? I've noticed promising results in the last few months and expect further growth in the near future.

* * *

Action step

Remember a specific time when you gave up prematurely on a goal. Imagine how things could have been different if you had used *The Law of Patience* and note this in your **Action Guide** (*Part III. Section XVI. The Law of Patience*).

18

THE LAW OF LONG-TERM THINKING

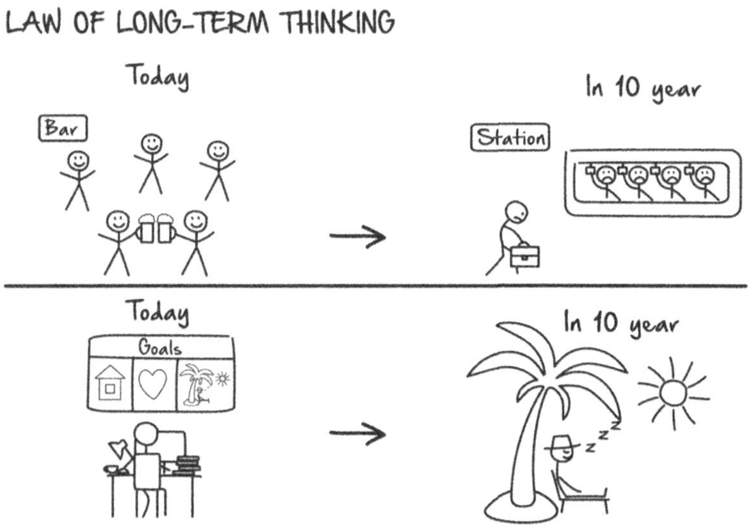

> The only thing worse than being blind is having sight but no vision.
>
> — Helen Keller, author.

The Law of Long-Term Thinking states that as you develop the habits of long-term thinking, you will become far more successful in *all* areas of your life.

One of the best predictors of success is your ability to think long term. Highly successful people project themselves into the future *all the time.* They hold a compelling vision they can't wait to make happen and move toward their goals with enthusiasm, confidence and determination. They follow a clear, written plan to reach their vision.

In his book *Goals!* the success expert, Brian Tracy, wrote:

"Dr. Edward Banfield of Harvard University concluded, after more than fifty years of research, that "long-time perspective" was the most important determinant of financial and personal success in life. Banfield defined long-time perspective as the "ability to think several years into the future while making decisions in the present."

"Average" people, on the other hand, seldom think in the long term. They're more concerned with receiving their paycheck at the end of the month or getting the latest technological gadget than they are about planning for their future. These people are unable to delay instant gratification and make sacrifices in the short term in order to gain everything they want in the long term. Sadly, over the course of their lives, they will have spent more time making grocery lists than they did on writing plans for the future.

What about you? How often do you project yourself one year into the future? Five years into the future? Twenty years into the future?

Your ability to think long term is an excellent indicator of your potential future level of success. If most of the things you do every day aren't activities you'll reap benefits from in the long term—whether it is investing your money, pursuing a worthy cause or taking care of your health—I seriously encourage you to rethink what you do.

Let me say it again. One of the main reasons people fail to achieve their goals is because they don't focus enough on the long term. You *must* develop the habit of continuous long-term thinking.

If you constantly think three or five years down the road and act every day in accordance with your long-term plan, you cannot fail to achieve significantly better results than you would while concentrating on the short term. This is inevitable.

The main characteristics of a long-term thinker

Do you often think of your ideal future? Do you take the necessary actions every day to make it a reality? Below are a few characteristics exhibited by people who think long-term:

- **They have a clear vision for their future:** They understand the power of clarity and know what they want their life to look like in five years, ten years or even longer.
- **They have a clear written long-term plan:** Successful people don't just fantasize about a hypothetical future, they are crystal-clear in what they want, and then they create a specific plan of action to make the vision a reality. They're practical dreamers.
- **They take their goals very seriously:** They don't just set goals and forget about them. They review their goals on a regular basis, often daily.
- **They're future-oriented:** They think of their future all the time and are continuously excited about their vision. They spend very little time thinking of the past except to learn from their failures.

So, how well do you fare on each of the above points?

Remember, successful people have a long-term vision they consistently move toward. They wake up knowing what they have to do that day and keep heading in the direction they've chosen. Unsuccessful people, on the other hand, let external circumstances decide what their future is going to be.

Are you using each day to build your future?

What you do every day is either moving you closer to your ideal future or away from it. To design the life you want, you must spend a majority of your time working on tasks aligned with your long-term vision.

A key question I encourage you to ask yourself is, "If I keep doing what I'm doing today or this week, will I achieve my long-term vision?"

For instance:

- Is what you're working on today aligned with your vision?
- Does what you're eating today reflect the vision you have for your long-term health?
- Is the way you're managing your money today contributing to your future finance the way you like?

It sounds obvious, but if what you do every day isn't aligned with your vision, you will probably never achieve it.

The importance of having a compelling vision

Your ability to think long term is directly linked to your vision. One reason successful people constantly project themselves into the future is that their vision is huge, and they know it will require years of hard work before coming to fruition. What allows them to stay focused on their long-term vision is their level of clarity regarding what they want (the power of clarity) and the compelling nature of their vision (the power of passion).

Similarly, the clearer and more compelling your vision is, the easier it will be for you to focus on the long term.

Also, note that a big and compelling vision requires you demand more of yourself. Bestselling author, Brendon Burchard, has identified raising your standard as a key component of success. For instance, studies have shown that students perform above the norm when teachers expect more from them. This is known as the "Pygmalion Effect" and demonstrates that teachers' expectations influence their students' performance. The results of an experiment lead by Rosenthal and Jacobsen at an elementary school showed that students who were believed to display "unusual potential for intellectual growth" ended up scoring significantly higher when tested eight months later. The only issue is that they were selected randomly, not because of an unusual potential as teachers had been made to believe.

Similarly, if you set a compelling vision and decide you *must* raise your standards to perform at the highest level you possibly can, over the long term you'll improve significantly more than you otherwise would, perhaps even beyond your imagination.

The key is to believe you can improve regardless of your external circumstances. This is what Carol Dweck describes in her book, *Mindset*, as adopting a "growth mindset," as opposed to having a "fixed mindset," which means, holding the belief you can't improve.

Think long term and imagine yourself becoming one of the best in your industry within the next decade or two. Make it your responsibility to excel at whatever you do, whether it is to serve more people more effectively or to take better care of your family or community. Remember, someone with no compelling vision will seldom—if ever—excel at what they are doing.

We all know people who have been playing the same sports for decades as a hobby. Now, have any of them become world-class players? Of course, not. They wouldn't even do that with as many hours of practice as professional players. Why? Because their intent wasn't to become the best they can. Their intent was purely to play for enjoyment.

Unless you commit to raising your standards, you'll never uncover what you're capable of becoming. I encourage you to think bigger, be bolder and continuously seek clarity regarding what you want out of life.

If you're interested in raising your standards and becoming your best self, I encourage you to refer to my book, *Upgrade Yourself: Simple Strategies to Transform Your Mindset, Improve Your Habits and Change Your Life.*

Is your vision big enough?

Are you pursuing a compelling vision that keeps you awake at night and makes you jump out of your bed every morning?

One way to assess the size of your vision is to look at what you focus on. Are you merely focused on yourself, or are you thinking about what you can do for others? What do you say when you talk about your vision and what questions do you ask others? Do you ask vague and insipid questions, or do you ask powerful questions that reflect your ambitious vision? For instance, if you want to be a coach and serve people, which of the following questions would you ask a coach:

- How can I become a coach?
- How can I become one of the best coaches in the world?

Look at the type of questions you ask yourself and others. What do they say about the size of your vision?

Are your problems big enough?

The size of your vision also determines the size of your challenges. Do you think someone whose mission is to change the world focuses on petty things? Small people usually have small problems, while big people have big problems. If you keep worrying about minor issues that won't matter tomorrow or next week, it shows that your thinking is too small. As the size of your vision grows and your perspective on life changes, most of your small problems will vanish. You will stop paying them attention because you'll be thinking at a different, more significant level.

Your ability to act with the big picture in mind is critical. You need to set a long-term vision that excites you and use this excitement to raise your standards. Remember, the difference between high achievers and "average" performers is often that the former set a clear compelling vision for their lives and commit to making it happen at all costs.

* * *

Action step

Answer the following questions using the **Action Guide** (*Part III. Section XVII. The Law of Long-Term Thinking*):

- Will what you're doing today, or this week, allow you to achieve your long-term goals?
- What are you thinking about throughout your day? Make a list of some of the recurrent thoughts you entertain every day. Are they aligned with your long-term vision?
- What questions are you asking yourself and others? Are they empowering you or are they limiting your chances of achieving your goals?

In the next section, we'll discuss how to build emotional resilience in greater detail.

PART IV

BUILDING EMOTIONAL RESILIENCE

1

THE IMPORTANCE OF EMOTIONAL STABILITY

> Success consists of going from failure to failure without loss of enthusiasm
>
> — Winston Churchill

Life is made of ups and downs. One day you feel amazing and ready to conquer the world, the next day you feel terrible, wondering what you're doing with your life. To achieve your goals, you must be able to stick to the process for long enough, regardless of external circumstances. You must learn to trust the process, knowing that if you keep doing what you have to do every day, you will eventually obtain the results you want. You must remain consistent over time even when everything around you seems to fall apart. In many cases, this is what separates successful and unsuccessful people.

To remain stable, you must learn to control your emotions. People enslaved by their emotions will seldom find the discipline needed to do the things they know they should be doing. They will fall prey to negative emotions, giving up their goals prematurely.

On the other hand, if you can win the inner game and manage your emotions better, you will be able to achieve almost anything you want.

Most of the laws and principles in this book will help you take control of your mind which, in turn, will help you achieve your long-term goals.

Remember, you are your own worst enemy. More than anybody else, *you* are the one standing in your own way and sabotaging your efforts. Learn to control your thought processes and emotions, and you will be more likely to achieve your long-term goals.

* * *

Action step

Rate yourself on a scale of 1 to 10 (1 being false, 10 being true) on the following points in your **Action Guide** (*Part IV. Section I. The Importance of Emotional Stability*):

1. I prepare myself for the worst and have contingency plans for my goals.
2. When I commit to something, I do it regardless of the way I feel.
3. I learn from each of my failures, and I am rarely affected by them.
4. I never beat myself up when things don't go as planned.
5. I'm self-compassionate and seldom blame myself or feel as though I'm a failure.
6. I cultivate gratitude every day.
7. My environment empowers me to be my best self.

Preparing for the worst

Who do you think is the most likely to succeed? The person who thought everything would be easy and the journey was going to be a breath of fresh air? Or the one who realized there would be tons of obstacles along the way and mentally prepared themself for that?

When you set goals, it is essential you prepare yourself effectively. Your ability to imagine the worst and prepare for it will dramatically enhance your chances of success. It will also help you manage difficult times even more effectively.

You *must* paint a picture that is as close as possible to reality. In fact, I encourage you to paint an even gloomier picture. By envisioning the worst, you'll be far better equipped to deal with future setbacks and be much more likely to achieve your long-term goals.

For instance, when I started my online business, I envisioned the worst-case scenarios:

- My blog being hacked leading to the loss of all my articles.
- My Amazon KDP account being stolen resulting in the loss of my books.
- Not making any money for several years.

I intentionally forced myself to imagine the worst, which served me well. In June of 2017, my six-year-old computer broke down and I lost all the data on it, including two books I had finished writing. Thanks to the mental preparation I had completed beforehand, this event didn't affect me much, and I was able to rewrite those two books from scratch. One of my friends who is also a writer told me he would have committed suicide if the same thing had happened to him. Hopefully he was joking, but it does demonstrate the power of mental preparation.

A 4-step process to prepare yourself mentally

To strengthen your mental resilience, I invite you to follow the process below:

1. Write down the worst-case scenarios.

What would be the absolute worst nightmare? Just imagine the worst and write anything that comes to mind.

2. Visualize yourself experiencing these scenarios.

If the worst-case scenarios were to happen, how would you feel? What kind of thoughts would cross your mind? Visualize yourself experiencing them as vividly as possible.

3. Write down what you would do to overcome these challenges.

For each scenario, write down briefly what you would, or could, do to overcome these challenges.

4. Ask yourself what you're willing to endure before giving up.

What would make you give up on your goal? Deciding when to give up will help you persevere. As long as the conditions aren't met, you simply *have* to keep going.

* * *

Action step

Go through the 4-step process using the **Action Guide** (*Part IV. Section I. The Importance of Emotional Stability*).

2

OVERRULING YOUR FEELINGS

> I think self-discipline is something, it's like a muscle. The more you exercise it, the stronger it gets.
>
> — Daniel Goldstein

You are *not* your emotions. Sadly, most people act and react based on their emotions, failing to grasp this simple truth. They never realize they can overrule their emotions and take control of their destiny.

One effective way to start taking control of your emotions is through total commitment. Once you know what you want and commit to it, your emotions take second place, thereby losing some of their power. Commitment forces you to overcome negative emotions, such as fear, and to eliminate all your excuses so you can move toward your goal with much more conviction and determination.

In his book, *6 Months to 6 Figures*, Peter Voogd introduces a key concept he calls, "The Decision Train." With it, he argues that most people's way of making decisions is as follows:

Feelings > Actions > Decisions.

Here is how it works: people feel a certain way and, as a result, take a certain type of action, which translates into their final decision.

For instance, if they don't feel like working, they procrastinate, if they don't want to go to the gym, they skip it, and if they have no desire to wake up early, they sleep in.

On the other hand, the five percent, as Peter Voogd calls them, rely on the following decision train:

Decisions > Actions > Feelings

That is, regardless of how they feel, they make a decision first, then they follow through by taking the appropriate action and, as a result, they feel great about themselves.

For instance, they decide to write a book this year, complete it and feel wonderful as a result. Or they commit to exercise three times a week consistently and feel proud of it.

Do you see how overruling your feelings can allow you to build more self-discipline while stabilizing the chaotic process that success can often be?

I rely on this type of commitment to help me accomplish all my challenging goals. When I told my father my goal to write eight books this year, he asked me how I could come up with so many book ideas, but this is largely irrelevant to me. Why? Because I decide my goal first, then I find a way to achieve it. In short, I utilize the following process:

- **Decisions:** I decide what I will do and commit to it (writing eight books this year).
- **Actions:** I take actions (creating a writing schedule and sticking to it).
- **Feelings:** I feel good as a result (build more confidence and discipline as a result of achieving my goals).

To tell you the truth, I don't know what my next book will be about. I'll think about it while finishing this one. My point is, I don't rely on luck or inspiration to reach my goals. Instead, I set a goal, commit to it and then find a way to achieve it. Then, I follow the most effective process I know of until I achieve my goal (see also *The Law of Effective Action*).

Please note, the goals I commit to are process goals—goals I have control over—not result goals over which I have only limited control. For instance, writing eight books is a process goal as it is almost entirely within my control. However, selling 10,000 copies of my books isn't. I have only partial control over this (although there are a lot of things I can do to promote and sell more books).

Remember, emotions fluctuate. You can overcome emotional rollercoasters by realizing you are not your emotions and by committing to well-defined processes and process goals. Your ability to overrule your feelings will allow you to achieve far better results than is otherwise the case.

* * *

Action step

Write down the following on a piece of paper or print out the corresponding page in your **Action Guide** and put it on your desktop where you can see it (*Part IV. Section II. Overruling Your Feelings*):

Decisions > Actions > Feelings

3

REFRAMING

> Failures, repeated failures, are finger posts on the road to achievement. One fails forward toward success.
>
> — C.S. Lewis, British novelist

Another way to achieve better control of your emotions is to shift your perspective and reframe the way you perceive negative events, thereby giving them a more empowering meaning. To learn more, you can refer to my book, *Crush Your Limits.*

We all react to events based on our experiences and our lifelong social conditioning. This is the main reason why you can put two people in the exact same situation and one will be happy while the other will be miserable. The happiest and most successful people use reframing to give a much more empowering meaning to life events.

Rethinking failures

For most people, failure is something to be avoided. And sadly, school does a bad job of teaching children how to deal with failures. In truth, what constitutes a failure is largely subjective. You can change the way you perceive failures by shifting your perspective on them.

The way you experience life is shaped by the way you relate to various concepts such as success, happiness, money and work. Your life can be negatively impacted if you happen to hold limiting beliefs or incorrect assumptions regarding any of these concepts. For example:

- If you think success is an event rather than a process, you'll likely fail to achieve your long-term goals.
- If you believe money is the root of all evil, you might struggle financially for the rest of your life, because who wants to admit to yearning for an evil?
- If you believe happiness is having a bigger house and a nicer car, you may end up living a rather unhappy life.

What you believe about key concepts has tremendous consequences.

Failure is also a concept. It can mean different things to different people. In fact, to achieve your goals you'll have to try many things and many of these won't work. This is how the process we call success works. Now, whether you choose to see these events as failures or not is subjective.

To reframe failures and deal with them more constructively, it is essential you give them a more empowering meaning. After all, everything is a matter of perspective. Here are some of the things that may affect your perspective on failures:

- **Biology:** fear of rejection is a big threat. In the past, being rejected from a tribe could severely reduce the chance of survival. As a result, nowadays we tend to avoid situations that could lead to public humiliation or criticism. This often limits our willingness to try new things lest we look bad.
- **Social conditioning**: social conditioning plays a large part in the way you perceive failure. When you were a kid, you may have been ridiculed when you failed to do something, or you may have witnessed other people being made fun of. Over time, you've learned to associate failure with pain.
- **Expectations:** for failure to exist there must be boundaries between what constitutes a failure and what doesn't. These boundaries result from your expectations. For instance, imagine

you set a goal of losing twenty pounds by the end of the year and make it clear that you will settle for nothing less than that. In that case, if you end up losing only five pounds, you may see it as a total failure. From an objective point of view, however, it could also be interpreted as a positive result—you actually lost five pounds.

- **Lack of understanding:** the more you see so-called failures as part of the process that leads to the achievement of your goals, the less they will be perceived in a negative light. Failure and success are part of the same process, not separate from it.
- **Level of identification with failures:** failing to achieve something doesn't make you a failure. You merely tried something that didn't work. In fact, no amount of failure can fundamentally change the essence of who or what you are. Failures become less painful as you learn to separate your actions and behaviors from your identity. If something didn't work as planned, don't see yourself as a failure. Instead, reflect on your actions and behaviors and ask for feedback. Then, start again, but this time, make changes. As Einstein once said (and I paraphrase slightly), the definition of lunacy is repeating the same thing and expecting different results.
- **Timeframe:** your relationship with failure is greatly affected by the way you position an event in the big picture of your life. Put simply, a failure is less significant when seen as part of a long-term vision. For instance, if you give yourself three years to lose thirty pounds, losing "only" six pounds this year is not something you'll perceive as a failure, because you still have two more years to reach your desired weight. Similarly, if you estimate it will take you five years to create a business, failing the first year will have less of a negative impact than if you give yourself only two years. The more long term you can think, the less short term "failures" matter.

Changing the meaning

Two people can experience the same event and interpret it in two radically different ways. The farmer may celebrate the onset of rain while the picnickers may curse it. It all depends on your perception of the event.

The way you interpret an event leads you to have certain thoughts, which creates emotions that drive you to take a particular action. Thus, if you want to change the way you respond to an event, you must start by changing the way you interpret it.

For instance, if every time something doesn't work you say to yourself, "I'm a failure," you'll experience negative emotions such as feelings of inadequacy, which may lead you to stop working on your goal. On the other hand, if you perceive failures as opportunities to learn, you'll be in a much more positive emotional state. Rather than ruminating on the event, you will be able to learn from it, so you can achieve better results next time.

Here is a great question to help you reframe a potentially negative situation, "What's great about it?"

This question always allows you to shift your perspective and focus on the positive side of things. If you can't think of anything, then ask yourself, "What *could* be great about it?" If you had to find something positive about an event that happens to you, what would it be?

For instance, let's say you got fired from your job. Obviously, this is a stressful event. But what could be great about it? Try it out yourself. Imagine you've just been laid off from your current job. What's great about it? How can you reframe that event so it empowers you to move forward?

What did you come up with?

Perhaps it gives you an opportunity to do something you've always wanted to try, but never dared to. Or it may give you a chance to move to another industry you've always been interested in. It could also provide you with more time to work on creating a small business.

The ability to reframe what happens is a powerful way to give meaning to seemingly meaningless or unfair events. In his classic book, *Man's Search for Meaning*, psychologist, Viktor E. Frankl, relates his experience in a concentration camp during the Second World War. He considers meaning to be one of the main reasons he was able to survive in such a cruel environment. Below is a great example of the reframing he used with one of his clients:

"Once, an elderly general practitioner consulted me because of his severe depression. He could not overcome the loss of his wife who had died two years ago and whom he had loved above all else. Now, how could I help him? What should I tell him? Well, I refrained from telling him anything but instead confronted him with the question, "What would have happened, Doctor, if you had died first, and your wife would have had to survive you?" "Oh," he said, "for her this would have been terrible; how she would have suffered!" Whereupon I replied, "You see, Doctor, such a suffering has been spared her, and it was you who have spared her this suffering—to be sure, at the price that now you have to survive and mourn her." He said no word but shook my hand and calmly left my office. In some way, suffering ceases to be suffering at the moment it finds a meaning, such as the meaning of a sacrifice."

Whether you face somewhat inconsequential setbacks or incredibly challenging times, learn to reframe the situation and to give it an empowering meaning that will allow you to keep going. If you look hard enough, you can find a positive meaning in everything. It's not what happens that determines the major part of our life, it's the meaning we create out of what happens and the action we take as a result of our interpretation.

* * *

Action step

Think of one major failure you had in your life. Now, come up with as many empowering meanings as you can and write them down using your **Action Guide**. What's great about the event? What did/could you learn from it? (*Part IV. Section III. Reframing*).

4

OVERCOMING CHALLENGING TIMES

> Our ability to handle life's challenges is a measure of our strength of character.
>
> — LES BROWN, MOTIVATIONAL SPEAKER

One of the biggest problems people face is managing themselves during challenging times. You may be motivated to work on your goals when everything goes well, but you can easily become miserable when things don't go as planned.

What you do when facing setbacks or experience negative emotions is fundamental to your success. In this section, I will underline common pitfalls that may prevent you from achieving your long-term goals. By learning how to avoid these pitfalls, you'll be able to manage your emotions more effectively and persevere for longer.

1. Avoid the "I already screwed up" excuse

Many people are excited at the beginning of the journey. They joined the local gym or started a new promising diet, feeling more motivated than ever. However, after a few weeks, they become disheartened and fall off track. Perhaps their diet was going well but on a stressful day, they binge ate. Now they beat themselves up, blaming their lack of self-discipline. Then, they think, "I already failed, so I can eat anything I want. Screw the diet."

This type of black and white approach to goal setting can lead many people to sabotage their efforts. It comes from the belief that, if we are not consistent one hundred percent of the time, we are failing. Success, however, is a process and, as such, isn't black and white. It is far more nuanced and includes both successes *and* so-called failures.

A great analogy is the stock market. If you studied the fluctuations of the stock market over the past hundred years, you'll notice a general upward trend. Now, is it always going up? Of course not. There are ups and downs and sometimes even big crashes. But temporary downward trends don't prevent the stock market from increasing over the long term.

The same principle applies in your life. Binge eating one day doesn't prevent you from achieving your long-term weight-loss goal. Neither is skipping the gym for a week an invitation to screw up the past three months you spent working out! Avoid interpreting temporary setbacks as a means to beat yourself up. Instead, give yourself some slack and remember, success is a process and, therefore, takes time. As one of my friends once told me, life is a marathon, not a sprint, and self-compassion, not self-criticism, is the fuel you need to keep going long term and finish the race.

Thus, be extra careful whenever you notice you're falling off track. It doesn't mean you're a "failure" and is certainly not an invitation to blame yourself and give up. Remember, your ability to manage your feelings will determine for a large part whether you'll achieve your goals in the long term. It's easy to feel motivated when things go well. The real test is what you do when they aren't.

Realize success is a long-term, and often chaotic, process that includes multiple "failures" along the way. Keep focusing on the long term and cut yourself some slack when things don't work out exactly as planned. This will greatly increase your odds of achieving your goals.

2. Adopt an "I'll beat myself up later" mindset

The worst time to make a decision is when we're in a negative emotional state. Yet, this is when most people make poor decisions, such as giving up. The temptation to beat ourselves up can be high and, for some reason, we often enjoy playing the victim and derive a perverse pleasure when we inflict mental pain upon ourselves.

To avoid such situations, I encourage you to adopt an "I'll beat myself up later" mindset. In other words, whenever you feel down, avoid judging yourself and avoid making any decision that could have a negative impact in the long term. For instance, the worst time to give up on your goals would be when you feel discouraged or depressed. Always wait until you're in a positive mental state before making any important decision. Meanwhile, be self-compassionate, accept that disappointment is part of the process and hang in there. You'll have plenty of time to beat yourself up later when you feel better. But for now, give yourself a healthy dose of compassion.

3. Perform damage control during tough times

Remember, failures and disappointments are both part of the success process, not separate from it. The question is not whether you'll have challenging times, but how you'll deal with them. Rather than trying to avoid negative emotions, actively work to limit their impact and shorten their duration. If you can accept they are part of the process, you'll be far more likely to succeed long term.

4. Overcome recurrent negative thought patterns

We all buy into a specific story we call "our life." This story is made up of recurrent thought patterns. For instance, you probably have a few negative thought patterns that lead you to feel sad or depressed from time to time. It could be the, "I'm not good enough," "I'm worried about money," or "I'm not disciplined enough," pattern. If you recall, the 80/20 rule states that twenty percent of your actions leads to eighty percent of your results. It also works for your emotions. Twenty percent of your negative thought patterns can create eighty percent of your suffering. Your job is to identify what these specific thought patterns are and act to alleviate them.

Once you've identified the negative twenty percent, you want to look at the thought process behind them. What kind of thoughts are leading you to experience these negative emotions? Try to be as specific as possible.

After having identified these thoughts, ask yourself, "What underlying beliefs lead me to have these thoughts in the first place?"

Then, challenge each of these beliefs.

Finally, come up with new empowering thoughts you can focus on whenever your negative thoughts kick in. By doing so consistently, you will start weakening your negative thought patterns and create new empowering ones.

For example, one negative thought I often have is the fear of not making it as a full-time author. This manifests whenever things don't work out the way I want them to. It could be when I'm launching a new book and sales don't hit the stratosphere, when my overall sales drop or just when such negative thoughts occur randomly during the day.

While I always do my best to ignore these thoughts whenever they arise, sometimes they do trigger negative emotions. When it happens, I focus on positive thoughts that give me the confidence I will succeed as a writer. For instance:

- I think of all the successful authors in my genre. Especially, self-published authors. Sometimes, I even write down their names.
- I remind myself thousands of authors are successful, and I'm as capable as any of them.
- I remember I still have plenty of time and show a great deal of self-compassion. I also remind myself of my *Bullet-Proof Timeframe*, knowing all I have to do for now is to write. I can worry about the outcome later.
- I tell myself I can always improve my writing since I've only been an author for a few years.

- I reread all my book reviews and comments from people who told me I'm "on the right path" and should "keep inspiring the world."

You might want to think of this process as "closing a sale." When you try to sell a product or service to someone, they often come up with objections. Now, image if you knew each of these objections by heart. Wouldn't it be easier to close the sale? Similarly, if you have dozens of counter-arguments you can use when your negative thought patterns kick in, you'll find it easier to overcome these patterns and limit the negative impact they have on your life.

Note that the new empowering thoughts you use as counter-arguments can turn into deeper beliefs if you create a habit of focusing on them each day. This could be by repeating affirmations for instance (for more on this see *The Law of Conditioning*).

* * *

Action step

Go through the process below using the **Action Guide** (*Part IV. Section IV. Overcoming Challenging Times*):

- Remember a time you gave up on one of your goals. Visualize yourself encountering a similar situation in the future. Now, see yourself acting with self-compassion.
- Whenever you experience negative emotions, give yourself some slack and wait until you feel better before making any important decisions.
- Identify recurrent negative patterns.
- Write down a few negative thought patterns that lead you to experience negative emotions.
- Go one step further now and identify the specific thoughts and images that go through your mind.
- Ask yourself, "What would I need to believe in order to experience these thoughts?"

- Come up with new empowering thoughts (counter-arguments) and use them when your negative thought pattern kicks in.
- Turn these new empowering thoughts into powerful beliefs through daily conditioning.

5

CULTIVATING SELF-COMPASSION

> Remember, you have been criticizing yourself for years and it hasn't worked. Try approving of yourself and see what happens.
>
> — Louise L. Hay, motivational author and founder of Hay House

Self-compassion beats self-criticism

For some reason, we like to blame ourselves whenever we fail to live up to our own high expectations. Even when we have every reason to be happy, our mind seems to be seeking ways to move away from that state of happiness. This is because our brain is not designed to make us happy but to ensure our survival. In addition, we often allow ourselves to be happy only up to a certain point before reverting to our natural happiness "set-point." To overcome these natural tendencies, it is important we choose to focus on the positive side of things.

Self-compassion is an effective way to deal with self-criticism and prevent unnecessary suffering. It can help you persevere during challenging times and reduce self-sabotaging behaviors. While you may believe you need to be hard on yourself to avoid slacking off, research has shown that self-criticism is, in fact, a subpar strategy in the long run. In, *The Willpower Instinct,* psychologist, Kelly McGonigal, wrote the following regarding self-criticism:

"If you think that the key to greater willpower is being harder on yourself, you are not alone. But you are wrong. Study after study shows that self-criticism is consistently associated with less motivation and worse self-control. It is also one of the single biggest predictors of depression, which drains both, "I will" power and "I want" power. In contrast, self-compassion—being supportive and kind to yourself, especially in the face of stress and failure—is associated with higher motivation and better self-control.

Here is a truth: self-compassion is more powerful than self-criticism. Thus, don't be afraid to be self-compassionate. It will serve you well long term.

Remember, self-compassion is an important component of the *Self-Empowerment Triangle* we discussed earlier. The more self-compassion you develop, the better you'll perform (and feel) in the long term.

Why sucking at most of the things you do is fine

We often have a specific image of how we should be and beat ourselves up when we fail to meet that standard. We also tend to compare ourselves with others, which can easily create feelings of inadequacy, even though these comparisons are unfair almost all the time.

There are many things you can't do well. And that's how it should be. This is why people specialize in different things. Thus, whether you're terrible at cooking, driving, writing or singing, it isn't an issue. Neither is having no sense of humor, zero public speaking skills or little charisma a problem in itself.

In truth, you can absolutely design a great life all the while doing a poor job at most of what you do. And what's the point in blaming yourself for things you cannot do anyway?

Often, the reason you're not good at something is merely that you lack the experience. If that's the case and if you wish to become better, the simple answer is to gain more experience.

Also, bear in mind you don't need to improve at everything you do. Sometimes, accepting your weaknesses and focusing on your strengths is a much better strategy. Being exceptional at a couple of things can often be enough to build a great career and a great life, not to mention it can also be far more enjoyable. The last thing you want is to spend your life doing things you're incompetent at. It will not only be exhausting, but it will also do a disservice to people who could benefit from your actual talents and strengths.

In short, when it comes to things you do poorly, you can do one of the following things:

- Accept completely your incompetence and be fine with it.
- Create a plan of action to become better (if you wish to).
- Ask someone else to do it for you.

Whatever option you choose is fine. There is no need to blame yourself or compare yourself to others because you can't do X, Y or Z. You just have to do one of the three points mentioned above and move on.

Avoiding the "I'm not good enough" trap

Even high achievers feel as though they aren't good enough and constantly try to prove themselves to the word. When they fail to live up to their expectations, they beat themselves up.

Wanting to become better isn't necessarily about trying to be good enough, though. It is about loving the process and feeling good about yourself as you become better each day. It doesn't come from a place of lacking, but from a place of curiosity and a desire to contribute more.

You can achieve great things while enjoying the journey. Seeking continuous growth while acknowledging your progress—as opposed to never feeling good enough—is possible. To do so, you must adopt the regular habit of celebrating your small wins. Unless you take the time to pat yourself on the back and savor your successes, you run the risk of feeling insecure and chronically dissatisfied.

To enjoy the journey, you need to realize this simple truth: you can always improve. You don't have to live in the future, hoping one day you'll make it. You don't need to suffer because you're not there yet. Where you are now in terms of skills and abilities is *exactly* where you're supposed to be. That's what we call "reality."

The first step is to acknowledge this undeniable truth and accept it completely. Doesn't it make you feel lighter to recognize you don't need to be there (yet), but can be happy here right now? The second step is to understand you can always grow and learn. The third step is to remind yourself you have time. You have years to improve and master whatever skills you want to master. The fourth and final step is to realize that becoming better over time is inevitable. If you follow the process in this book, you *will* become better. It *is* inevitable.

So, if you've told yourself, "I'm not good enough," replace this belief with, "I'm not as good as I want to be *yet,* but I'm good enough *for now.*"

The words "yet" and "for now" may seem insignificant, but they make all the difference in the world. "Yet" makes you realize you can always improve and eventually you will. "For now" indicates you're exactly where you're supposed to be and invites you to acknowledge everything you're doing well *at the moment*.

* * *

Action step

Complete the corresponding exercises in the **Action Guide** (*Part IV. Section V. Cultivating Self-Compassion*).

6

PRACTICING GRATITUDE

> Just to give a glimpse into its benefits, gratitude increases self-esteem, enhances willpower, strengthens relationships, deepens spirituality, boost creativity, and improves athletic and academic performance.
>
> — Dr Robert A Emmons, author of "The Little Book of Gratitude"

Gratitude is one of the most powerful forces on earth. Your ability to be grateful for all the things you already have will make you happier and help you become more resilient during difficult times.

Most people have a myriad of reasons to feel grateful, but few really are. Instead of counting their blessings, they obsess over trivial things, and thereby make their lives miserable. Whereas they could bring their attention to what goes well, they choose to focus on what they lack, constantly looking for faults in themselves and in others. As the business philosopher, Jim Rohn, said, "*The poor pessimist leads an ugly life ... He looks through the window and doesn't see the sunset, he sees the specks on the window!*"

Life may not be easy, but is there any reason to make it harder by focusing on the negative?

In truth, we've never had access to so many services in all of human history. Having food, shelter and a few trusted friends alone should already be enough to live a good life. Yet most of us take these things for granted, seeking happiness in acquiring more things, such as a bigger house, a nicer car or fancier vacations. While those are fine, why look for more if we aren't satisfied with what we already have? It is important to note that a poor person who cultivates the daily habit of gratitude will, over time, be happier than most rich people ever will.

How to develop gratitude

Have you ever felt sad or depressed, while nothing in the external world actually changed? This could be because of what you focus on.

For the most part, your ability to feel grateful results from what you choose to focus on in your daily life. If you focus on all your problems, you can quickly become depressed. On the other hand, if you look for wonderful things to be grateful for, you'll experience a deeper sense of gratitude.

To make my day more manageable when I was an unhappy employee, I would spend fifteen to thirty minutes every morning performing gratitude exercises.

Now, you might wonder how you can cultivate a deeper sense of gratitude, and I can tell you, the answer is simple: by practicing. Make it a habit to practice gratitude every morning. This way, you'll set yourself up for a great day. Below is a roundup of what I like to do when I wake:

- I close my eyes, think of someone, thank them and remember one or two things they have done for me. For instance, it could be advice they gave me or a lesson they taught me. I repeat the process with the next person who comes to mind. You don't need to choose anyone in particular. Just let your mind wander. To elicit deeper feelings of gratitude, I like to listen to beautiful songs while doing this exercise. Consider doing this exercise for at least a couple of minutes each day.

- I read through my gratitude journal. This journal contains nice comments, compliments and book reviews I received. In my mind, I go through some of the entries and thank people for their support.

While this is what I personally do, many other ways are possible. For instance, you could:

- Write down things you're grateful for.
- Look at an object, think of all the people involved in its creation and fully appreciate how lucky you are to have such a thing.
- Ask yourself what you're grateful for and answer that question out loud. Try to come up with as many things as you can.
- Remember all the things that went well today before going to bed.

The wonderful thing about these exercises is that they give you a sense of control over your life. You can choose to do these exercises daily and look for the good, instead of letting your mind and external circumstances dictate your emotional state.

Practicing gratitude will make you happier and will strengthen your emotional resilience. This, in turn, will help you stay consistent over the long term, preventing you from giving up on your goals prematurely.

Remember, your capacity to deal with negative emotions will help you achieve your long-term goals. This is one of the fundamental components of success. Therefore, learn to see the glass as half full, and don't forget, there are always things to be grateful for.

What will you do every day to experience more gratitude and make your life even more precious?

* * *

Action step

Select one gratitude exercise from the **Action Guide** and stick to it for the next two weeks (*Part IV. Section VI. Practicing Gratitude*).

7

LEVERAGING THE POWER OF PROXIMITY

> You must surround yourself with people who see greatness in you.
>
> — Bo Eason, formal American football player and speaker

Imagine if all your friends were highly successful. Do you think you would achieve better results?

What if you were around healthy, fit people? Would that help you lose weight?

You are largely the product of your environment. Your subconscious continuously absorbs vast amounts of information without your awareness. To design the life you really want, you must optimize your physical and social environment. It is far easier to be successful when you are surrounded by people who uplift you and expect the best from you, than when you are in a toxic environment surrounded by people trying to sabotage your efforts.

How to design an empowering environment

To optimize your environment and increase your chance of success you must do one or more of the following:

1. Improve the quality of your daily input (i.e., the information you consume).
2. Surround yourself with people who lift you up.
3. Design an empowering physical environment.

1. Improve the quality of your daily input

The information you consume every day greatly impacts your psychology. Listening to the news can make you fearful and create needless stress and worry. Equally, consuming motivational and educational resources can motivate you to become a better version of yourself.

I encourage you to begin and end your day on a positive note. This will help because your subconscious mind is more receptive in the morning after waking and at night before falling asleep, thus enabling you to reprogram your mind more effectively.

Below are some of the things you can do in the morning, in the evening or both:

Exercising: exercising has been shown to improve your mood. Some studies even show it can be as effective as anti-depressants. Take care, though—heavy exercise in the evening can negatively affect your sleep.

Consuming inspiration materials: creating a daily habit of reading inspirational books or watching motivational videos will help you create a more positive mindset.

Practicing gratitude: spending time every day to express gratitude is an effective way to enhance your well-being (see also *Practicing Gratitude*).

Meditating: meditation is a great way to calm your mind and reduce negative emotions. It also teaches you to observe your thoughts and take them less seriously.

Asking empowering questions: asking yourself empowering questions is a great way to shift your focus toward the positive things happening in your life. Here are some fantastic questions to ask yourself at the end of each day:

- What are the three things I'm proud of today? (This is a great way to build your self-esteem and train your mind to focus on small wins).
- What are the three things I did well today? (Same effect as above. There may be some potential overlap in your answers).
- What am I grateful for today?
- What could I have done *even* better today? Note, the importance of using "even." You want to acknowledge yourself for what you did and think of how you could have done an even better job. You don't ever want to beat yourself up.

A few tips on the above:

- Make sure you give specific answers.
- Force yourself to come up with answers even if they seem insignificant. Things you are proud of could be little things such as waking on time, not beating yourself up too much or eating fruit.
- At the end of each week, try to remember the answers you've made during the week. It will help you rewire your brain even further.

This exercise doesn't have to take more than a couple of minutes each day, but it can be very effective when practiced consistently for an extended period. First, commit to doing it for two weeks and see the results you achieve.

2. Surround yourself with people who lift you up

People you hang out with most of the time will greatly determine your future. Needless to say, negative people with bad habits, poor self-discipline and little self-awareness will drag you down.

In fact, as we have seen, negativity usually wins over positivity. One negative person in a group of five positive people tends to have a greater negative influence on the whole group than a positive person will have in the reverse situation. This is why it is so important you surround yourself with positive people who encourage you to raise your standards.

Realize that your environment beats your willpower, because you're immersed in your environment 24/7, while your willpower requires a conscious effort and will inevitably diminish over time.

Continuously try to surround yourself with successful people who have already achieved the goals you seek to achieve. They will challenge you to raise your standards and, over time, you will naturally copy their mindset and adopt similar beliefs.

3. Design a physical environment to empower you

Your physical environment also has a massive influence and tends to be more powerful than your willpower. A good example is the way your physical environment affects your diet.

I've noticed the power of my environment on my diet when, in a rare moment of weakness, I caught myself eating nuts that were on my desk. As I put them in my mouth, I suddenly realized how mechanical the act was.

This is why you won't find any sweets or sugary drinks in my home or office (I have a sweet tooth). If I want to eat something sweet, I'll have to go out and buy it. By the way, as I'm editing this book, my internet modem is hidden in a drawer in another room. This way, I can stay focused on my work.

Here is another example of how your physical environment can affect your behavior:

Imagine your fridge is full of cans of your favorite drink. Every time you open your fridge, you have to exert willpower to refrain from grabbing one. You may also see your family members grabbing one, perhaps they'll even leave a bottle on the kitchen table.

In this example, it's as if your environment were screaming at you, "Go for it. Have that drink." At the end of the day, when you feel tired and have depleted your willpower, you won't be able to resist grabbing one can from the fridge. And it's no wonder!

When it comes to the principle of proximity, the rule of thumb is:

- Make it as difficult as possible to indulge in behaviors or activities you want to avoid.
- Conversely, make it as easy as possible to adopt desirable behaviors or activities.

Below are a few examples of what you can do to design a more empowering environment that supports your goals:

- **Remove all distractions from your workspace:** get rid of your smartphones and any documents or items on your desktop except for the ones you absolutely need. The added benefit of this method is that it primes your mind by telling you, "Now I'm working".
- **Sort out files on your computer and make sure you can access all the files you need immediately.**
- **Eliminate all unhealthy food from your home and replace it with healthy foods:** for instance, you could have a basket of fruit available in several strategic places.
- **Prepare your running gear the day before:** this will make it as easy as possible to go for a run whenever you want to.

To sum up, to leverage the *Power of Proximity,* you must make sure the things you need to improve your life are:

1. Around you
2. Close to you
3. As easy as possible to access, and/or
4. Automatized (through daily rituals).

* * *

Action step

Write down the things you will do to create a more empowering environment using the **Action Guide** (*Part IV. Section VII. Leveraging the Power of Proximity*).

PART V

WORKING WITH OTHERS

1

ADDING VALUE TO PEOPLE'S LIVES

> In our interviews, we found that high performers give an extraordinary amount of thought to questions of service: how to add value, inspire those around them and make a difference. Their attention in this area could best be described as a search for relevance, differentiation and excellence.
>
> — Brendon Burchard, High Performance Habits.

The million-dollar question

Have you ever experienced a sense of joy after donating money to charity? Have you ever felt valued after using your knowledge to help others?

While we tend to focus on our selfish needs, helping others can be far more powerful and beneficial in the longer term. Not to mention that it makes us feel good about ourselves.

In fact, experiments have shown that spending money on others tends to make us happier than spending it on ourselves. Thus, as much as we like to think of humans as selfish, this is not necessarily the case. In fact, if anything, helping others seems to be wired in our brain as a way to ensure the survival of the community. Yet, ironically, we tend to shy away from doing so, focusing instead on our own needs.

Here is the million-dollar question that I encourage you to keep asking for the rest of your life: "How can I help you?"

Constantly focusing on ways to help others, whether it is your family members, your friends, your colleagues or complete strangers, is one of the most powerful habits you can develop. I've found that if you're willing to go the extra mile to support others, they will almost automatically return the compliment in the future. Giving is one of the most effective ways to develop meaningful relationships in your personal and professional life.

Put yourself in other people's shoes

Understanding what people want and helping them get it, is one of the best things you can do to ensure your own long-term success. Practice seeing things from other people's perspectives. Discover their aspirations. Then, help them achieve their goals. If you can do this, they will likely go above and beyond to help you get what *you* want. Or, as the famous motivational speaker, Zig Ziglar, once said, "*You can have everything in life you want, if you will help other people get what they want.*"

To identify other people's needs, you must understand the following:

- **Their career goals:** what do they want from their career? Do they want to grow their business? Earn a promotion?
- **Their issues:** what key issues are they facing in their lives right now?
- **Their vision:** what is their ultimate vision? Understanding other people's vision is critical. Once you know what they want to accomplish, it becomes easier to help them in a meaningful way.
- **Their values:** knowing their values will help you better understand the decisions they make. The more values you have in common, the easier it will be to build a meaningful relationship.

- **Their hobbies:** what do they enjoy during their spare time? Knowing their hobbies can help you identify some commonalities. You may even be able to help teach them something or share with them valuable resources.

Realize that most of the things you'll achieve in life, you'll need the help of other people. Thus, your ability to serve others and add value to their lives, whether they are clients, family members, friends or colleagues, will determine for the most part how successful you will be in all areas of your life.

How are you helping your spouse, your family, your friends or your colleagues achieve their goals? Do you even know what their goals are in the first place?

Focus on building long-term relationships

Most people mainly focus on the short term. They often hold a specific idea of how they want the other person to help. For instance, they may connect with them right before a new project hoping to receive their help. Or, to put it differently, they tend to prioritize the short term rather than seeing how the relationship could evolve long term.

However, it is far more effective to think of people you want to connect with as future friends you plan to hang out with for years. With such a mindset, you're coming from a place of helpfulness. Instead of trying to get something from them, simply connect with them, help them whenever you can and allow the relationship to evolve naturally from there.

After all, when you try to make new friends, you don't start by asking them for help or try to sell them something right away, do you? No. You learn more about them, look for common interests and see how you can create a win-win relationship, that is, a relationship you both want to be part of.

Learn to see others for what they could be

When you look at people, do you see their potential or their shortcomings? Do you encourage them to become more, or do you treat them as if they were doomed to stay forever where they are?

Successful people often make you feel you can accomplish far more than you believe possible. Small people, on the other hand, keep reminding you that your dreams are impossible, and you have little or no potential.

To help others more effectively you must see them for what they could be. Empowering them to grow will not only increase the odds they achieve *their* goals but also the odds *you* will achieve *yours*. This is because the more positive impact you have on other people, the more they will be willing to support you. Additionally, the more you can help others succeed, the more resources—influence, money, knowledge—they may have to support you in the future.

So, learn to believe in others. Refuse to see them as less than they can be. By doing so, you'll encourage them to improve their standards and achieve better results. In return, they will thank you by helping you.

Five tips to effective networking

Here's how you can use the information mentioned above to network more effectively:

1. **Listen attentively:** when networking, most people try to sell their products and services to someone they don't even know. Don't do that. Instead, learn to listen and show interest in what the other person is doing. Listen more than you talk and ask questions. A good rule of thumb is to avoid mentioning what you do before being asked. As Dale Carnegie wrote in his classic book, *How to Win Friends and Influence People*, "*You can make more friends in two months by becoming interested in other people than you can in two years by trying to get other people interested in you.*"

2. **Help others:** constantly seek to help people. Do so before asking for anything. If you know someone helpful you could introduce them to, let them know. If you have ideas that could help grow their business, tell

them. The more you provide value to others, the more likely they are to help you in the future. In his book, *Influence*, Robert Cialdini identifies "reciprocity" as one of the rules we can all use to influence others. Use it to your advantage by genuinely seeking to help others first.

3. **Aim to build long-term relationships:** approach any relationships with the desire to make a new friend for life, which entails being genuinely interested in the other person rather than pushing your own agenda down their throats.

4. **Look for commonalities:** as you communicate with someone you'd like to network with, whether in person or via email, look for things you have in common. Do you have similar values or areas of interest? Do you share common goals or hobbies? Obviously, the more you have in common, the easier it is to create rapport.

5. **Focus on creating win-win relationships:** avoid trying to take from people. Instead, constantly seek to create a win-win relationship. To do so, make sure you understand what the other person is looking for and what their long-term vision is. If you can help them, whether by introducing them to someone, sharing your knowledge or offering something of value to their clients, they'll be keen to work with you.

* * *

Action step

Complete the corresponding exercise in the **Action Guide** (*Part V. Section I. Adding Value to People's Lives*).

2

DEVELOPING AN ASKING MENTALITY

> To be successful, you have to ask, ask, ask, ask, ask!
>
> — Jack Canfield, Success coach and best-selling author

Have you ever asked your boss for a pay rise? Did you ask that person you like out on a date? Have you reached out to the guy who has the career you want? If not, why not?

I often see people limiting themselves by failing to ask, and I'm certainly guilty of that, too. We seem to talk ourselves out of asking for what we want for fear of rejection, or disturbing people, or because of pride or simply because we believe it is not okay to ask for what we want.

The problem is, if you don't ask the answer will never be yes. There are over seven billion people on this planet and you're rarely more than one click away from most of them. Among them, millions have the resources you need to achieve your goal, whether it is money, time or important connections. Why not ask for their help?

There is a myth we can do things on our own without any help from others. This is reflected in the common expression "self-made millionaire." However, in truth, most of the things we accomplish, we do so with either the direct or indirect help of others. Self-made millionaires are nothing without their customers, the knowledge they acquired in books written by others or the technologies they use in their business. And what about the support they received from family and friends?

We are all interconnected, and the idea we can do things on our own is an illusion. It only appears that way because we generally fail to acknowledge how much we benefit from the work of others. For instance, without Amazon, you wouldn't be able to read this book. But, in turn, Amazon couldn't operate without its tens of thousands of employees, and all of this is made possible thanks to the internet.

The bottom line is, you cannot do things just on your own. It is not only okay, but it is *necessary* you ask other people for help. Learn to ask for help and you'll dramatically enhance your chances of success.

Remember, people are often more than willing to help you. As we discussed earlier, human beings are hardwired to help each other. We tend to feel good and valued when we're offered the chance to help other people. So why not let other people help you?

I want you to develop an asking mentality and create a habit of asking others for help whenever necessary. As success coach, Jack Canfield, wrote in his book, *The Success Principles*, "*Learn to become an askhole*". His popular book, *Chicken Soup for The Soul*, was rejected by 144 publishers before being published. Jack Canfield is definitely a big *askhole*. The worst that can happen when you ask is that people will say "no," but by failing to ask, you say "no" to your dreams.

Imagine how your life could change if you were to ask the world for what you want. What would you ask for and from whom? Would you ask for a pay increase? Would you try to get someone to mentor you? Would you ask the special person you fancy out on a date?

If you want to know how to develop an asking mentality in greater detail, refer to my book, *The Passion Manifesto: Escape the Rat Race, Uncover Your Passion and Design a Career and Life You Love.*

* * *

Action step

Answer the following question in your **Action Guide** (*Part V. Section II. Developing an Asking Mentality*):

What is one thing you could ask for but, so far, haven't dared to?

PART VI

BONUS

1

FIVE CORE BELIEFS TO ACHIEVE SUCCESS

We have covered the *Seventeen Laws of Success* and discussed the importance of developing emotional resilience. We've also seen the habits you can develop to receive people's support. Now, let's look at some core beliefs to help you build confidence so you can achieve your goals. These are core beliefs that I've been relying on myself over the past few years.

If you want to discover even more core beliefs that will help you change your life, I encourage you to check out my book, *Crush Your Limits*. In it, you'll learn how to replace disempowering beliefs with new empowering ones that will impact your life in a positive way.

Belief #1—If one, then one million

This is one of the core beliefs running through the back of my mind. Below are some examples:

- If I can sell one book to one person, then I can sell one million books to one million people. It is just a matter of finding a way to reach them.
- If I can make one dollar online, then I can repeat the process and make $100, $1,000, $10,000, et cetera.

- If I can find one client, I can find many more.

Can you see how powerful this belief is? Instead of doubting myself, as many people do, I merely seek to make my first sale or find my first client. Then, I know ninety percent of the work is done. From this point onward, I know I will be able to repeat the process. I just have to persevere and make necessary adjustments along the way.

Belief #2—If others can, I can

This is another simple, yet incredibly powerful belief I hold. I always assume that if other people can, then I can (and I will).

- If others are making money online, I can.
- If others are making a living as self-published authors, I can.
- If others are retiring early, I can.
- If others are having it all, I can.

The truth is that what other people can do, in most cases you can also do. This belief can boost your confidence and bring more certainty in your ability to reach your goal. For me, as soon as I see thousands of people around the world succeed at something, I know I can and will achieve the same goal, if:

- I apply the processes in this book, and
- I'm passionate enough about what I'm doing.

In short, I always assume that what others can do, I can, too. It may take tons of work and require more time than for other people but, eventually, I will achieve similar results.

What if you adopted the belief that what others can do, you can, too? How much more certainty and confidence would it give you? What different actions would you take, starting today?

Belief # 3—I can get better

That's the whole point of this book, but let's repeat it: you *can* get better. In fact, as you practice the exercises in this book, getting better is inevitable. Keep practicing and learn from all your failures and you *will* improve.

I used to beat myself up for not being good enough, but then I realized something very powerful. Whatever I do right now is exactly what I'm supposed to. This is reality. *I'm good enough for now* and I can and will get better if I keep practicing.

In short, I shifted my focus from short- to long-term thinking. I gave myself some slack and reminded myself that I have time. The realization that I'm exactly where I'm supposed to be right now allowed me to relax more and stop beating myself up.

I now believe I can get better in each area of my life. I can overcome any major obstacle along the way, and so can you. After all, if other people can, I can. How? By practicing consistently, remaining patient and by managing challenging times effectively.

Belief # 4—Others will give up, therefore, I will succeed

Many people will give up after encountering major setbacks. Few will have the perseverance to "fail" again and again and keep going until they achieve the results they want. Most of my competitors aren't really my competitors, because I know they will give up at some point, while I will keep going and improving until I achieve my goal. Understand that your ability to stay focused on the process despite all the inevitable ups and downs will contribute significantly to your long-term success (see also *The Law of Perseverance*).

Belief # 5—Success is inevitable

Success is inevitable. That's a mantra I've been repeating to myself every day. I chose to believe success is inevitable because, after reading countless self-help books, I realized that, what determines our level of success is, for the most part, our belief in ourselves and in our visions.

In truth, I wasn't always confident in my ability to achieve my goals. Like most people, I doubted myself. However, as I kept progressing toward my goals, I developed more confidence in myself and in my vision. I did so by adopting new empowering beliefs like the ones in this section.

While I repeatedly failed to reach my targets, I still achieved many goals. I also adopted a morning ritual I stuck to every day for over six months. This discipline boosted my self-confidence. By shooting YouTube videos, doing Facebook Live and joining the public speaking group, Toastmasters, I expanded my comfort zone further building confidence.

By developing more confidence, you will be able to achieve most of your goals. And once you believe success is inevitable, giving up becomes irrelevant. You stop caring what people say you can and cannot do. Instead of worrying about the "how," you focus on the "why" behind your goals, trusting you are resourceful enough to solve any problem. Temporary "failures" become learning experiences you can use to reach your long-term goals. You come to realize that as long as you keep going, the game is still on. Life is a marathon, not a sprint. You have years to become better.

CONCLUSION

Thank you for purchasing this book and staying with me until the end. By doing so, you've already shown your commitment to transform your life. I applaud you for that.

You now understand at a much deeper level how success works. I encourage you to refer to this book as many times as necessary until you've become living proof of each of the concepts discussed in it. Remember, nothing changes until you do. Go deeper with everything you do and never forget that you can always become better. Keep improving until you become a master. If you can do this every day while remaining focused on your long-term vision, you'll be well on your way to designing and living a great life.

Also, understand that so-called failures are part of the process. Success is inevitable, but so is the occasional failure. On your journey toward your goals, you are likely to fail many times. Often, you will doubt yourself and will feel like giving up, but when this happens, keep focusing on the process and do what you have to do every single day. The ability to remain consistent regardless of external situations will allow you to achieve your goals in the long term.

Finally, if you believe this book can benefit people around you, make sure to tell them about it.

If you have any questions or want to share your story with me, you can contact me at any time at thibaut.meurisse@gmail.com. I love hearing from my readers.

All the best with your future goals.

Thibaut Meurisse,

Founder of Whatispersonaldevelopment.org

What do you think?

I want to hear from you! Your thoughts and comments are important to me. If you enjoyed this book or found it useful **I'd be very grateful if you'd post a short review on Amazon.** Your support really does make a difference. I read all the reviews personally so that I can get your feedback and make this book even better.

Thanks again for your support!

OTHER BOOKS BY THE AUTHORS:

Crush Your Limits: Break Free from Limitations and Achieve Your True Potential (Free Workbook Included)

Goal Setting: The Ultimate Guide to Achieving Life-Changing Goals (Free Workbook Included)

Habits That Stick: The Ultimate Guide to Building Habits That Stick Once and For All (Free Workbook Included)

Master Your Emotions: A Practical Guide to Overcome Negativity and Better Manage Your Feelings (Free Workbook Included)

Master Your Motivation: A Practical Guide to Unstick Yourself, Build Momentum and Sustain Long-Term Motivation

Productivity Beast: An Unconventional Guide to Getting Things Done (Free Workbook Included)

The Greatness Manifesto: Overcome Your Fear and Go After What You Really Want

The One Goal: Master the Art of Goal Setting, Win Your Inner Battles, and Achieve Exceptional Results (Free Workbook Included)

The Passion Manifesto: Escape the Rat Race, Uncover Your Passion and Design a Career and Life You Love (Free Workbook Included)

The Thriving Introvert: Embrace the Gift of Introversion and Live the Life You Were Meant to Live (Free Workbook Included)

The Ultimate Goal Setting Planner: Become an Unstoppable Achiever in 90 Days or Less

Upgrade Yourself: Simple Strategies to Transform Your Mindset, Improve Your Habits and Change Your Life

Wake Up Call: How To Take Control Of Your Morning And Transform Your Life (Free Workbook Included)

ABOUT THE AUTHOR

THIBAUT MEURISSE

Thibaut Meurisse is a personal development blogger, author, and founder of whatispersonaldevelopment.org.

He has been featured on major personal development websites such as Lifehack, Goalcast, TinyBuddha, Addicted2Success, MotivationGrid or PickTheBrain.

Obsessed with self-improvement and fascinated by the power of the brain, his personal mission is to help people realize their full potential and reach higher levels of fulfillment and consciousness.

In love with foreign languages, he is French, writes in English, and lived in Japan for almost ten years.

Learn more about Thibaut at:

amazon.com/author/thibautmeurisse

whatispersonaldevelopment.org
thibaut.meurisse@gmail.com

MASTER YOUR EMOTIONS (PREVIEW)

> The mind in its own place, and in itself can make a heaven of Hell, a hell of Heaven.
>
> — JOHN MILTON, POET.

We all experience a wild range of emotions throughout our lives. I had to admit, while writing this book, I experienced highs and lows myself. At first, I was filled with excitement and thrilled at the idea of providing people with a guide to help them understand their emotions. I imagined how readers' lives would improve as they learned to control their emotions. My motivation was high and I couldn't help but imagine how great the book would be.

Or so I thought.

After the initial excitement, the time came to sit down to write the actual book, and that's when the excitement wore off pretty quickly. Ideas that looked great in my mind suddenly felt dull. My writing seemed boring, and I felt as though I had nothing substantive or valuable to contribute.

Sitting at my desk and writing became more challenging each day. I started losing confidence. Who was I to write a book about emotions if I couldn't even master my own emotions? How ironic! I considered giving up. There are already plenty of books on the topic, so why add one more?

At the same time, I realized this book was a perfect opportunity to work on my own emotional issues. And who doesn't suffer from negative emotions from time to time? We all have highs and lows, don't we? The key is what we *do* with our lows. Are we using our emotions to grow? Are we learning something from them? Or are we beating ourselves up over them?

So, let's talk about *your* emotions now. Let me start by asking you this:

How do you feel right now?

Knowing how you feel is the first step toward taking control of your emotions. You may have spent so much time internalizing you've lost touch with your emotions. Perhaps you answered as follows: "I feel this book could be useful," or "I really feel I could learn something from this book." However, none of these answers reflect how you feel. You don't 'feel like this,' or 'feel like that,' you simply 'feel.' You don't 'feel like' this book could be useful, you 'think' this book could be useful, and that generates an emotion which makes you 'feel' excited about reading it. Feelings manifest as physical sensations in your body, not as an idea in your mind. Perhaps, the reason the word 'feel' is so often overused or misused is because we don't want to talk about our emotions. So, how do you feel now?

Why is it important to talk about emotions?

How you feel determines the quality of your life. Your emotions can make your life miserable or truly magical. That's why they are among the most important things to focus on. Your emotions color all your experiences. When you feel good, everything seems, feels, or tastes better. You also think better thoughts. Your energy levels are higher and possibilities seem limitless. Conversely, when you feel depressed, everything seems dull. You have little energy and you become unmotivated. You feel stuck in a place (mentally and physically) you don't want to be, and the future looks gloomy.

Your emotions can also act as a powerful guide. They can tell you something is wrong and allow you to make changes in your life. As such, they may be among the most powerful personal growth tools you have.

Sadly, neither your teachers nor your parents taught you how emotions work or how to control them. I find it ironic that just about anything comes with a how-to manual, while your mind doesn't. You've never received an instruction manual to teach you how your mind works and how to use it to better manage your emotions, have you? I haven't. In fact, until now, I doubt one even existed.

What you'll learn in this book

This book is the how-to manual your parents should have given you at birth. It's the instruction manual you should have received at school. In it, I'll share everything you need to know about emotions so you can overcome your fears and limitations and become the type of person you really want to be.

You'll learn what emotions are, how they are formed, and how you can use them for your personal growth. You'll also learn how to deal with negative emotions and condition your mind to create more positive emotions.

It is my sincere hope and expectation that, by the end of this book, you will have a clear understanding of what emotions are and will have all the tools you need to start taking control of them.

More specifically, this book will help you:

- Understand what emotions are and how they impact your life
- Identify negative emotions that control your life and learn to overcome them
- Change your story to take better control over your life and create a more compelling future, and
- Reprogram your mind to experience more positive emotions.

Here is a more detailed summary of what you'll learn in this book:

In **Part I**, we'll discuss what emotions are. You'll learn why you are wired to focus on negativity and what you can do to counter this effect.

You'll also discover how your beliefs impinge upon your emotions. Finally, you'll learn how negative emotions work and why they are so tricky.

In **Part II**, we'll go over the things that directly impact your emotions. You'll understand the roles your body, your thoughts, your words, or your sleep, play in your life and how you can use them to change your emotions.

In **Part III**, you'll learn how emotions are formed. You'll also learn how to condition your mind to experience more positive emotions.

And finally, in **Part IV**, we'll discuss how to use your emotions as a tool for personal growth. You'll learn why you experience emotions such as fear or depression and how they work. You'll then discover how to use them to grow.

To start mastering your emotions today go to:

mybook.to/Master_Emotions

I. What emotions are

Have you ever wondered what emotions are and what purpose they serve?

In this section, we'll discuss how your survival mechanism affects your emotions. Then, we'll explain what the 'ego' is and how it impacts your emotions. Finally, we'll discover the mechanism behind emotions and learn why negative emotions can be so hard to deal with.

1. How your survival mechanism affects your emotions

Why people have a bias towards negativity

Your brain is designed for survival, which explains why you're able to read this book at this very moment. When you think about it, the probability of you being born was extremely low. For this miracle to happen, all the generations before you had to survive long enough to procreate. In their quest for survival and procreation, they must have faced death hundreds or perhaps thousands of times.

Fortunately, unlike your ancestors, you're (probably) not facing death every day. In fact, in many parts of the world, life has never been safer. Yet, your survival mechanism hasn't changed much. Your brain still scans your environment looking for potential threats.

In many ways, some parts of your brain have become obsolete. While you may not be seconds away from being eaten by a predator, your brain still gives significantly more weight to negative events than to positive ones.

Fear of rejection is one example of a bias toward negativity. In the past, being rejected from your tribe would reduce your chances of survival significantly. Therefore, you learned to look for any sign of rejection, and this became hardwired in your brain.

Nowadays, being rejected often carries little or no consequence to your long-term survival. You could be hated by the entire world and still have a job, a roof and plenty of food on the table, yet, your brain is still programmed to perceive rejection as a threat to your survival.

This is why rejection can be so painful. While you know most rejections are no big deal, you nevertheless feel the emotional pain. If you listen to your mind, you may even create a whole drama around it. You may believe you aren't worthy of love and dwell on a rejection for days or weeks. Worse still, you may become depressed as a result of this rejection.

In fact, one single criticism can often outweigh hundreds of positive ones. That's why, an author with fifty 5-star reviews, is likely to feel terrible when they receive a single 1-star review. While the author understands the 1-star review isn't a threat to her survival, her authorial brain doesn't. It likely interprets the negative review as a threat to her ego which triggers an emotional reaction.

The fear of rejection can also lead you to over-dramatize events. If your boss criticized you at work, your brain may see the event as a threat and you now think, "What if I'm fired? What if I can't find a job quickly enough and my wife leaves me? What about my kids? What if I can't see them again?" While you are fortunate to have such an effective survival mechanism, it is also your responsibility to separate real threats from imaginary ones. If you don't, you'll experience unnecessary pain and worry that will negatively impact the quality of your life. To overcome this bias towards negativity, you must reprogram your mind. One of a human being's greatest powers is our ability to use our thoughts to shape our reality and interpret events in a more empowering way. This book will teach you how to do this.

Why your brain's job isn't to make you happy

Your brain's primary job is not to make you happy, but to ensure your survival. Thus, if you want to be happy, you must take control of your emotions rather than hoping you'll be happy because it's your natural state. In the following section, we'll discuss what happiness is and how it works.

How dopamine can mess with your happiness

Dopamine is a neurotransmitter which, among other functions, plays a major role in rewarding certain behaviors. When dopamine is released into specific areas of your brain—the pleasure centers—you get a high. This is what happens during exercise, when you gamble, have sex, or eat great food.

One of the roles of dopamine is to ensure you look for food so you don't die of starvation, and you search for a mate so you can reproduce. Without dopamine, our species would likely be extinct by now. It's a pretty good thing, right?

Well, yes and no. In today's world, this reward system is, in many cases, obsolete. While in the past, dopamine was linked to our survival instinct, The release of dopamine can now be generated artificially. A great example of this effect is social media, which uses psychology to suck as much time as possible out of your life. Have you noticed all these notifications that pop up constantly? They're used to trigger a release of dopamine so you stay connected, and the longer you stay connected, the more money the services make. Watching pornography or gambling also leads to a release a dopamine which can make these activities highly addictive.

Fortunately, we don't need to act each time our brain releases dopamine. For instance, we don't need to constantly check our Facebook newsfeeds just because it gives us a pleasurable shot of dopamine.

Today's society is selling a version of happiness that can make us *un*happy. We've become addicted to dopamine largely because of marketers who have found effective ways to exploit our brains. We receive multiple shots of dopamine throughout the day and we love it. But is that the same thing as happiness?

Worse than that, dopamine can create real addictions with severe consequences on our health. Research conducted at Tulane University showed that, when given permission to self-stimulate their pleasure center, participants did it an average of forty times per minute. They chose the stimulation of their pleasure center over food, even refusing to eat when hungry!

Korean, Lee Seung Seop is an extreme case of this syndrome. In 2005, Mr Seop died after playing a video game for fifty-eight hours straight with very little food or water, and no sleep. The subsequent investigation concluded the cause of death was heart failure induced by exhaustion and dehydration. He was only twenty-eight years old.

To take control of your emotions, it is essential you understand the role dopamine plays and how it affects your happiness. Are you addicted to your phone? Are you glued to your TV? Or maybe you spend too much time playing video games. Most of us are addicted to something. For some people it's obvious, but for others, it's more subtle. For instance, you could be addicted to thinking. To better control your emotions, it is important to shed the light on your addictions as they can rob you of your happiness.

The 'one day I will' myth

Do you believe that one day you will achieve your dream and finally be happy? This is unlikely to happen. You may (and I hope you will) achieve your dream, but you won't live 'happily ever after.' This is just another trick your mind plays on you.

Your mind quickly acclimates to new situations, which is probably the result of evolution and our need to adapt continually in order to survive and reproduce. This is also probably why the new car or house you want will only make you happy for a while. Once the initial excitement wears off, you'll move on to crave the next exciting thing. This phenomenon is known as 'hedonic adaptation.'

How hedonic adaptation works

Let me share an interesting study that will likely change the way you see happiness. This study, which was conducted on lottery winners and paraplegics, was extremely eye-opening for me. Conducted in 1978, the investigation evaluated how winning the lottery or becoming a paraplegic influence happiness:

The study found that one year after the event, both groups were just as happy as they were beforehand. Yes, just as happy (or unhappy). You can find more about it by watching Dan Gilbert's Ted Talk, The Surprising Science of Happiness.

Perhaps you believe that you'll be happy once you've 'made it.' But, as the above study on happiness shows, this is simply not true. No matter what happens to you, you'll revert back to your predetermined level of happiness once you've adapted to the new event. This is how your mind works.

Does that mean you can't be happier than you are right now? No. What it means is that, in the long run, external events have very little impact upon your level of happiness.

In fact, according to Sonja Lyubomirsky, author of *The How of Happiness*, fifty percent of our happiness is determined by genetics, forty percent by internal factors, and only ten percent by external factors. These external factors include such things as whether we're single or married, rich or poor, and similar social influences.

This suggests, only ten percent of your happiness is linked to external factors, which is probably way less than you thought. The bottom line is this: Your attitude towards life influences your happiness, not what happens to you.

By now, you understand how your survival mechanism impacts negatively your emotions and prevent you from experiencing more joy and happiness in your life. In the next segment/section we'll learn about the ego.

To read more visit my author page at:

amazon.com/author/thibautmeurisse

ACTION GUIDE

PART I. Mastering the Four Powers That Enable Success

Defining success

What does success really mean to you? Write down your personal definition of success below:

I. The Power of Absolute Responsibility

If you were to take one hundred percent responsibility of your life, what is one thing you would start doing today to improve your life?

Write down your answer below:

II. The Power of Belief

You can dramatically increase your level of confidence by building self-discipline, boosting your self-esteem and enhancing your self-confidence

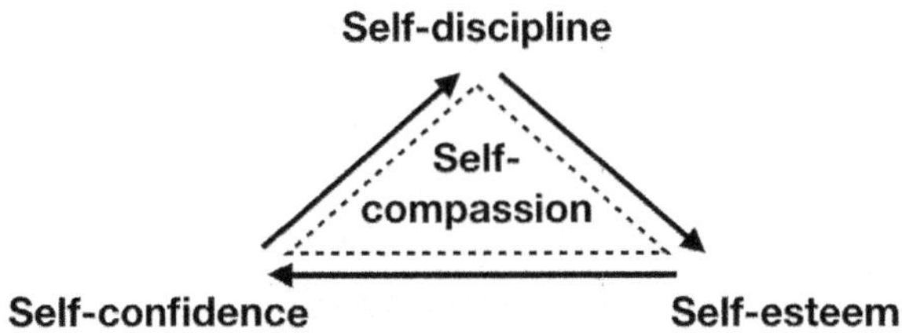

The Self-Empowerment Triangle

Building self-discipline

To build self-discipline consistency is key. Write down one thing you could start doing consistently every day for the next thirty day (meditating, practicing gratitude, setting goals etc.)

-

Boosting your self-esteem

Do at least one of the following exercises:

1. Ask yourself 3 things you want to acknowledge yourself for (for at least a week)
2. Write down all your accomplishments (at least once)
3. Reward yourself (select a reward for one of your goals)
4. Record every positive thing you've ever been said. (for at least a month)

Enhancing your self-confidence

Remain consistent with your new daily habit and keep acknowledging your small wins. Re-read the book and apply each law to the best of your ability.

III. The Power of Clarity

Rate yourself on a scale of 1 to 10 for the following, 1 being a big NO and 10 a big YES:

Career/mission: do you wake up excited? Dod you feel like you're making a difference in your own unique way?

1 10

Family: do you spend enough quality time with your family?

1 10

Finance: do you make the kind of money you want to make or do you struggle to make ends meet?

1 10

Health (Physical and emotional): Do you have a healthy body? How about your emotional well being?

1 10

Personal growth: do you feel like you're growing into the person you want to become?

1 10

Relationship: Is your relationship with your partner the best it could be?

1 10

Spirituality: do you feel a sense of connection with God/the universe?

1 10

For each area, take a few minutes to visualize in details what your ideal vision looks like. See yourself as being already at a 10 in each area and answer the question below:

- **Career:** What contribution are you making to society and the world in general? What does your day at work look like?
- **Family:** How are you interacting with your family on a day-to-day basis and how does that make you feel?
- **Finance:** How much money are you earning each month? What are you doing with this money?
- **Health:** How do you feel every day? What does your diet look like?
- **Personal growth:** What three words best describe you? What do people say about you when you're not there? What message are you spreading to the world?
- **Relationship:** What emotions are you experiencing daily? How

do you treat your partner? And how does him or her feel as a result of that? How does your partner treat you?

- **Spirituality**: How do you serve God or the universe? What spiritual qualities do you embody?

Your vision for your life

Write a short statement for each area of your life describing your ideal vision. For now, make sure you write at least one statement.

Career:

Family:

Finance:

Health:

Personal growth:

Relationship:

Spirituality:

The importance of self-awareness

Rate yourself for each statement below, 1 being false, 10 being true.

I know my core values and live by them

1 10

I know my weaknesses and cope with them effectively

1 10

I understand my core beliefs and how they affect my behaviors and actions

1 10

I've identified thought patterns that prevent me from reaching my potential

1 10

I've identified my zone of genius

1 10

I know whether I'm an extrovert or introvert and use it to my advantage

1 10

I control my emotions

1 10

I know my blind spots and seek new perspectives whenever necessary

1 10

I listen to my intuition

1 10

Now, look at your score for each statement and ask yourself, "What are the two things that, if I were to work on would make the biggest difference in my life?". Resolve to work on these two things using the exercises mentioned in the book.

2. Setting crystal clear goals

Select one major goal you want to achieve. (The one that would make the biggest difference in your life right now). Make it SMART and break it down into monthly, weekly and daily goals

For your reference SMART goals are:

- **Specific:** What exactly do you want? What are you trying to achieve?
- **Measurable**: Can you assess the progress towards your goal easily? How will you know whether you've achieved it?
- **Achievable**: Is it achievable? Is the timeframe realistic? Can you put in the effort required despite other responsibilities?
- **Relevant:** Is it in line with your values? Is it exciting you?
- **Time-bound:** Do you have a clear deadline for your goals?

For more on how to set goals, you can also check out my book *Goal Setting: The Ultimate Guide to Achieving Goals that Truly Excite You.*

Your SMART goals:

IV. The Power of Passion

Uncovering your passion

To help you clarify your passion, answer the following questions:

1. What did you enjoy doing when you were a kid?

2. Who do you envy? What are the people you envy doing?

3. If all your family members, friends and people you know were no longer around and you were all alone, what would you start doing from today?

4. If you had all the time and money in the world, what would you do?

5. If you had complete confidence and were already your absolute best self, what would you be doing with your life?

6. How do you want to express yourself to the world? Do you want to entertain, educate, inspire, heal, teach, or create? What emotions do you want people to feel as a result of the work you're doing?

For more on how to find your passion refer to *The Passion Manifesto: Escape the Rat Race, Uncover Your Passion, and Design a Career and Life You Love*

2. Strengthening your whys

Write down all the reasons why you *must* achieve your goal. To help you do so, you can use the four motivators: pain, pleasure, ego and love (You can write them in brackets after each of your reasons)

-

-

-

-

-

-

-

-

-

PART II. Activating the Power of Commitment

Rate yourself on a scale of 1 to 10, 1 being false, 10 being true.

I'm willing to learn whatever I need to learn to get where I want to be

1 10

I refuse to give up until I get the results I want

1 10

I constantly seek to raise my standards

1 10

I'm willing to swallow pride and use feedback to improve

1 10

What could you do to further commit to your goal? Write down at least one thing that could help you strengthen your commitment:

Remember, believing in yourself (power of belief), knowing what you want (power of clarity) and having a strong why (power of passion) will make it easier for you to commit. If you struggle to commit, look how well you fair for each of them.

Part III. Mastering the Laws of Success

I. The Law of Humility

By swallowing your pride and accepting to change everything needed to achieve your goals, you will dramatically increase the odds you succeed.

Write at least one reason pride could stand in your way. Answering the following questions might help you: How could pride prevent you from achieving the results you want in life? Do you refuse to ask for help? Are you unwilling to change things that don't work?

Your answer:

II. The Law of Mastery

If you apply anything you learn and go as deep as you can, you will inevitably get results long-term.

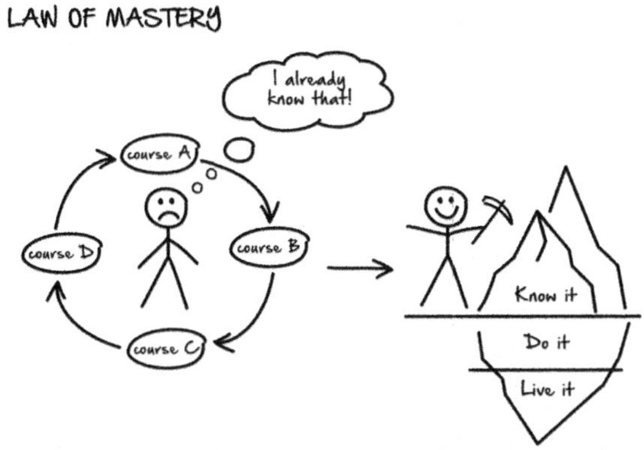

Developing a mastery mentality

On a scale of 1 to 10, 1 being false 10 being true, evaluate yourself on the following points:

I easily avoid jumping from one opportunity to another.

1 10

I put into practice everything I read or learn about.

1 10

When I learn something new I keep practicing until I reach a high level of mastery.

1 10

Look at one area of your life in which you aren't satisfied. How much of what you know have you actually put into practice? Have you mastered the fundamentals in this area?

1. Focusing on one thing at a time

Look at all the projects and goals you're working on right now. Now, select the one you're the most excited about and write it down. Turn it into a SMART goal and spend most your effort on it in the next few weeks or months *until* you get the results you want.

Your most exciting project:

Your SMART goal:

2. Practicing what you know intellectually

Write down all the things you know at an intellectual level but haven't truly mastered. That is, things you read or heard about but haven't really applied in your life.

-

-

-

-

-

-

-

-

-

-

3. Repeating the process until you reach a high level of mastery

Answer the following question: What one thing if you were to focus on until you master it, would make the biggest impact on your life?

III. The Law of Focus

Monomaniacal focus on the most important area of your life right now will yield great results while positively impacting most of the other areas of your life.

Among the five areas—health, finance, relationships, career, personal growth—which area, if you were to focus most of your effort right now, would help most transform your life?

IV. The Law of Effective Actions

Success becomes almost inevitable when you identify key actions and focus on them daily

Write down below what you could do to identify the strategic moves you need to adopt to achieve your goal. (Examples: find a role model, interview someone who has already achieved your goals etc.)

-
-
-
-
-
-
-
-
-
-

Brainstorm strategic move ideas.

Come up with at least 20 things you could do to achieve your goal:

-
-
-
-
-
-
-
-
-
-
-
-
-
-
-
-
-
-
-
-

Identify your strategic moves

What are three to five strategic moves that, if you were to focus most of your time and effort on would allow you to achieve your biggest goal?

1.

2.

3.

4.

5.

Apply the 80/20 rule

Use the 80/20 rule in one or several of the areas below:

Relationships: What are the few people who bring you most of your joy? How could you spend more time with them?

-

-

-

-

Happiness: What are the few things you derive most of your happiness from? What could you do to make them your main point of focus?

-

-

-

-

Work: What are the few tasks that really move the needle? How could you make them your priority?

-

-

-

-

Thoughts: What are the few thoughts that generate the most of your joy and excitement? What practice would allow you to consciously focus on these thoughts more often?

-

-

-

-

Worries: What are the few things you worry about that generate most of the stress you experience in your life? How you could eliminate these worries from your life?

-

-

-

V. The Law of Deliberate Practice

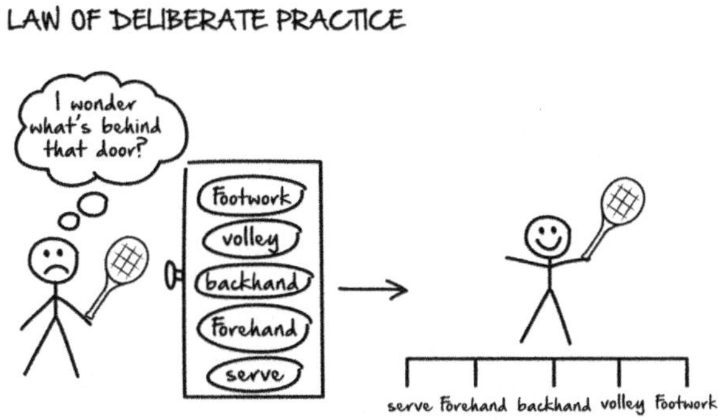

You'll become far more competent at what you do if you design effective practices aligned with your goals.

Apply deliberate practice to one of your goals by answering the questions below:

- Can you acquire the skills you need using effective training techniques that already exist? Y / N
- Does your current practice take place outside of your comfort zone? Y / N
- Does your current involve specific, well-defined goals? Y / N
- Does your current practice requires your full attention and conscious actions? Y / N
- Do you regularly ask for feedback? Y / N
- Does your current practice allow you to create and rely on effective mental representation? Y / N
- Does your current practice involves working on existing skills or building new ones by focusing on some aspects of those skills that need to be improved? Y / N

Based on your answers to the previous questions, write down what you could do specifically to improve the way you work on your goal:

VI. The Law of Consistency

Simple daily habits repeated for a few years lead to exceptional results, often far better than you would get by brute-forcing your way to success.

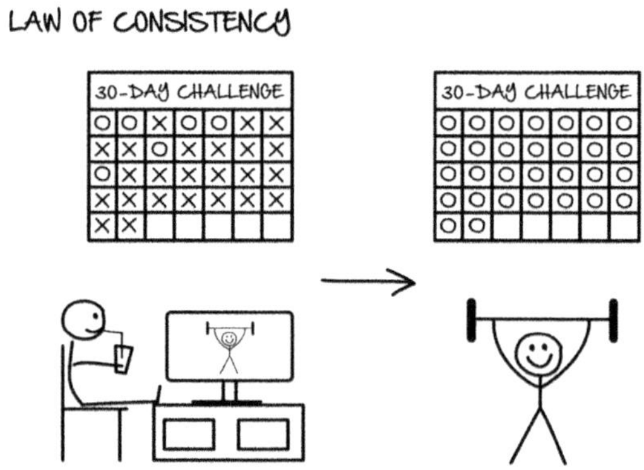

Turning strategic moves into daily habits

Look at the 3-5 strategic moves you've identified previously. Now, what could you do to turn them into daily habits?

Your daily habits:

Adoption one daily habit

Select one thing you could do first thing in the morning to help you achieve your main goals. Stick to it for at least thirty days.

Your daily habit:

VII. The Law of Identification

The more you think, feel and act like the person you wish to become, the faster you'll achieve your goals.

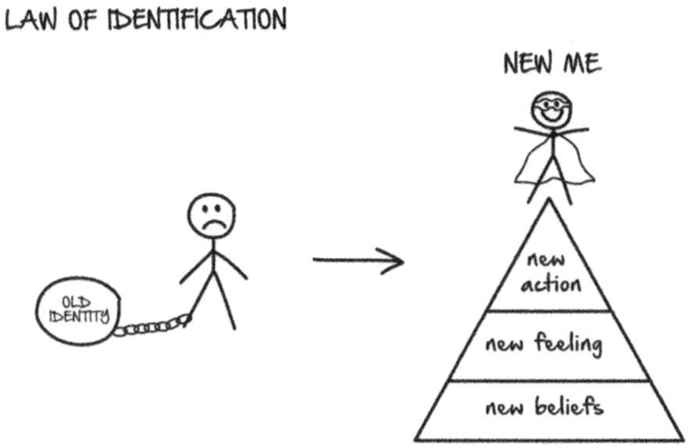

Write down below the side effects of having already achieved your goals:

1. What would be your core beliefs about yourself and about the world?

-

-

-

2. How would you think differently?

-

-

-

3. How would you feel?

-

-

-

4. What would you do differently?

-

-

-

5. What new habits would you have?

-

-

-

6. What old habits would you have rejected?

-

-

-

VIII. The Law of Conditioning

You can train yourself to experience any emotion if you focus on feeling that particular emotions for long enough.

Select one daily habit that will help you condition your mind to experience more positive emotions in your life. If you can, make it part of your morning ritual by combining it with the thing you committed to doing in the section *Law of Consistency*.

Your daily habit:

IX. The Law of Attraction

The more you focus on something, the more likely you are to attract that thing in your life.

Throughout your day, spend as much time as possible focusing on the main area you wish to make a change in. You can also repeat affirmations, visualize the results you want, write it down on a paper you put on your desk etc.

Write down below what you will stop focusing on (for instance: lack of money, past failures etc.). Then, cross out each element in your list.

-

-

-

-

-

-

-

-

-

Write down below the things you want to spend most of your time focusing on (what your grateful for, goals you want to achieve etc.). Underline each element in your list.

-

-

-

-

-

-

-

-

-

-

-

X. The Law of Reset

Every day is a new day independent of the previous one.

Do at least one of the following exercises:

1. Brainstorming exercise:

Write down everything you could do differently. Could you do something different upon waking up? Adopt one new positive habit in your life? Contact someone you haven't contacted for a while? Start journaling?

\-

\-

\-

\-

\-

\-

\-

2. 7-Day Challenge:

For the next seven days, begin your day as though you have been born again, and feel the field of possibilities ahead of you.

3. Visualization exercise:

Forget about everything—who you think you are, your past, your future etc.—and reconnect with the present moment. You can close your eyes to do this exercise. Now, spend a couple of minutes envisioning your future and what you want to create.

XI. The Law of Intent

The more purposeful you are during your day, the better results you will achieve.

Think of your typical day. What is the one segment of your day that if you could bring a specific intent to, would have the most positive impact? For the next seven days, resolve to set your desired intent before moving to that specific segment of your day.

Write down below the one segment of your day you want to change and how you want to feel during that time of the day.

Your segment of the day:

How you want to feel:

XII. The Law of Continuous Learning

Getting better is inevitable if you keep acquiring new skills and learn from failures. As you improve, long-term success becomes highly probable.

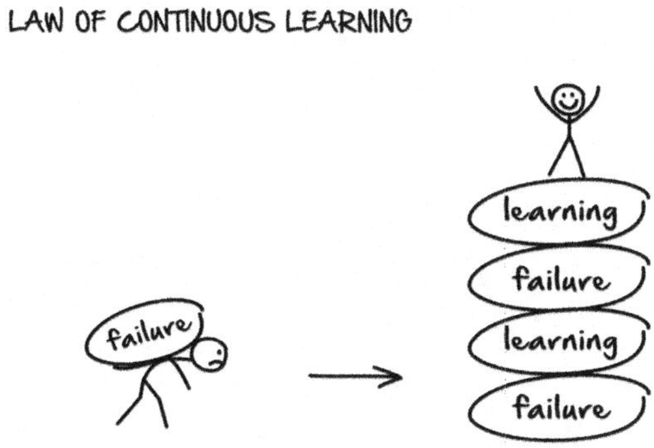

Commit to learning. Dedicate at least ten minutes daily to reading educational material that will help you achieve your long-term vision

XIII. The Law of Perseverance

You can and will achieve far more than you can ever begin to imagine if you keep persevering and refuse to give up prematurely.

Implement a Bullet-Proof Timeframe for your goal and commit to never giving up until you reach the deadline you chose.

Example: I'll keep writing books until April 18th, 2020.

Your Bullet-Proof Timeframe:

What you commit to doing by then:

XIV. The Law of Courage

The more often you can face your fear and move beyond your comfort zone, the more you'll achieve in life.

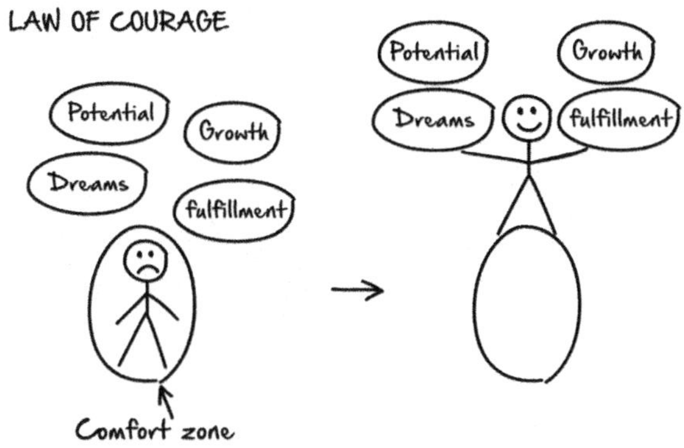

What is one thing you've been wanted to do for a while, but put off because of fear?

Could you challenge yourself and do that thing this week? Write down below one thing you could do to move beyond your comfort zone.

XV. The Law of Flexibility

The more you are willing to consider all the options available to achieve your goal, the more likely you are to succeed.

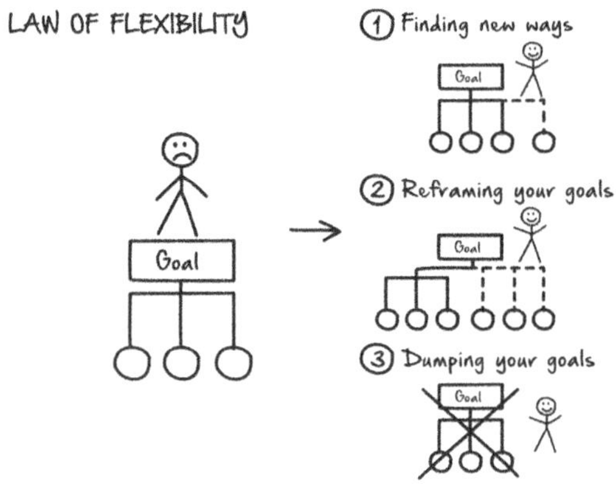

How could you use the Law of Flexibility to increase the chances that you achieve your long-term goals? Remember that you can identify additional ways to achieve your goals, reframe your goals or give up on your goals.

What are different ways you could achieve your goals?

-

-

-

-

How could you reframe your goal so that it opens the doors to new possibilities?

Does your goal still excite you or should you give up on it?

XVI. The Law of Patience

You must trust the process and remain consistent until you see the fruits of your labor.

Remember a specific time in the past when you gave up prematurely on a goal. Imagine how things could have been different if you had used the *Law of Patience.*

The one time I gave up prematurely:

XVII. The Law of Long-Term Thinking

As you develop the habits of long-term thinking, you'll become far more successful in all areas of your life.

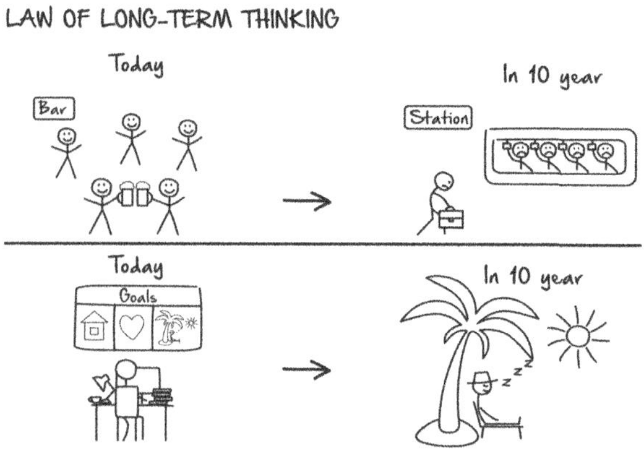

Write down your answers to the following questions:

Is what you are doing today or this week, will allow you to achieve my long-term goals?

c

What are you thinking about throughout your day? Make a list of some of the recurrent thoughts that you entertain every day. Are they aligned with your long-term vision?

-

-

-

-

-

-

PART IV. Building Emotional Resilience

I. The Importance of emotional stability

How resilient are you?

Rate the following statements on a scale of 1 to 10, 1 being false, 10 being true.

I prepare myself for the worst and have contingency plans for my goals.

1 10

When I commit to something, I do it regardless of the way I feel.

1 10

I learn from each of my failures and I am rarely affected by them.

1 10

I never beat myself up when I things don't go as planned.

1 10

I'm self-compassionate and seldom blame myself or feel.

1 10

I cultivate gratitude every day.

1 10

My environment empowers me to be my best self.

1 10

Go through the 4-step process below to strengthen your mental resilience

1. Write down the worst case scenarios.

What would be an absolute nightmare? Just imagine the worst and write anything that comes to mind.

2. Visualize yourself experiencing these scenarios.

If the worst case scenarios were to happen, how would you feel? What kind of thoughts would cross your mind? Visualize yourself experiencing them as vividly as possible.

3. Write down what you would do to overcome these challenges.

For each scenario, write down briefly what you would or could do to overcome these challenges.

4. Ask yourself what you're willing to endure before giving up.

What would make you give up on your goal? Deciding when to give up will help you persevere. As long as the conditions aren't met, you simply have to keep going.

II. Overruling Your Feelings

Write down the following on a piece of paper or print out the next page in your put it on your desktop where you can see it:

Decisions > Actions > Feelings

III. Reframing

Think of one major failure you had in your life. Now, come up with as many empowering meaning as you can and write them down. What's great about that? What did/could you learn from it?

-

-

-

-

-

-

-

-

-

IV. Overcoming challenging times

1. Remember a time you gave up on one of your goals. Visualize yourself encountering a similar situation in the future. Now, see yourself acting with self-compassion.

2. Whenever you experience negative emotions, give yourself some slack and wait until you feel better before taking any important decisions.

3. Identify recurrent negative patterns.

Write down a few negative thought patterns that lead you to experience negative emotions.

-

-

-

Go one step further now and identify the specific thoughts and images that go through your mind.

-

-

-

-

Ask yourself, "What would I need to believe in order to experience these thoughts?"

Come up with new empowering thoughts (counter-arguments) and use them when your negative thought pattern kicks in

Your empowering thoughts:

-

-

-

-

Turn these new empowering thoughts into powerful beliefs through daily conditioning.

Your powerful beliefs:

-

-

-

-

V. Cultivating self-compassion

Write down a few things you are poor at and that makes you feel bad about yourself:

-

-

-

-

-

-

Next to each of them write "Accept", "Act" or "Ask" in brackets.

"Accept" means you allow yourself to be poor at that thing and be fine with it.

"Act" means you want to do something to improve.

"Ask" means you'll ask someone to support you. It could be by delegating a certain task for instance.

Use the following statement whenever necessary:

"I'm not as good as I want *yet,* but I'm good enough *for now and I'm making progress*"

VI. Practicing Gratitude

Select one gratitude exercise below and stick to it for the next two weeks.

- Let your mind wander and thank people who come to mind
- Create a gratitude journal.
- Write down three things you're grateful for
- Look at an object, think of all the people involved in its creation and fully appreciate how lucky you are to have such an object.
- Ask yourself what you're grateful for and answer that question out loud. Try to come up with as many things as you can, or you could
- Remember all the things that went well today before going to bed.

VII. Leverage the Power of Proximity

Write down what you will do to create a more empowering environment.

Mental environment (What you put into your mind)

What you will do:

Social environment (Who you surround yourself with)

What you will do:

Physical environment (What is around you)

What you will do:

Part V. Working With Others

I. Adding value to people's lives

Adopt the following habits:

1. Constantly think of ways to help people around you

2. Put yourself in other people's shoes and seek to understand:

- Their career goals
- Their issues
- Their vision
- Their values
- Their hobbies

3. Learn to see others for what they can be.

II. Develop an asking mentality

Write down your answer to the following question:

What is one thing that you could ask for but haven't dared to?

Printed in Great Britain
by Amazon

48648747R00152